D1498795

A SOCIABLE GOD

A SOCIABLE GOD

---

*Toward a New Understanding
of Religion*

Ken Wilber

SHAMBHALA
Boston & London
2005

SHAMBHALA PUBLICATIONS, INC.
Horticultural Hall
300 Massachusetts Avenue
Boston, Massachusetts 02115
www.shambhala.com

9 8 7 6 5 4 3 2 1

Printed in the United States of America
♾ This edition is printed on acid-free paper that meets the
American National Standards Institute Z39.48 Standard.
Distributed in the United States by Random House, Inc.,
and in Canada by Random House of Canada Ltd

Library of Congress Cataloging in Publication Data
Wilber, Ken.
A sociable God.
p.   m.
Reprint. Originally published: New York: New Press, 1983
ISBN 0-394-72692-8 (pbk.)
ISBN 1-59030-224-9 (pbk. reissue: alk. paper)
1. Religion and sociology. 2. Psychology, Religious. I. Title. II. Series.
BL60.W53   1984   306'.684-5499

Contents

Foreword

OUR RELIGIONS, our Gods, and our selves may not be quite what we thought. That of course is nothing new. Indeed history can be read as an expression of their progressive evolution, as Ken Wilber has elegantly done in *Up from Eden*. For religion has been the driving force behind a vast range of behavior, calling forth the highest expressions of human nature and providing excuses for the lowest. Whole cultures have lived, killed, and died for their beliefs. Small wonder then that religion has been one of the central interests of psychology, sociology, and anthropology.

Throughout most of Western history religion was preeminent in defining our reality, and woe to the individual who suggested other views or even other methods of discovering truth (e.g., Galileo). Yet recent history, as if in recompense, has not been kind to religion; it has steadily lost ground to science and rationalism as the major purveyors of reality. Indeed, from the rational perspective, religion is frequently seen as a relic of prescientific thinking, an unfortunate carryover from less sophisticated times. God, if not dead, is at least moribund, surviving only through the unrequited longings of the psychologically immature.

Yet in recent years God has been staging a dramatic comeback, not only in traditional guise but in a full range of diverse forms, Eastern and Western, exoteric and esoteric, fundamentalist and gnostic. Christianity has seen both a fundamentalist revival and the reappearance of contemplative-mystical approaches. In addition, there has been an unprecedented influx of non-Western religions and disciplines—yoga, Zen, TM, and all. Some of these differ so fundamentally from our traditional beliefs and practices as to call into question some of our most basic assumptions about the very nature of religion itself. Buddhism, for example, posits no supreme being or God and centers around a rigorous program of mental training explicitly aimed at controlled psychological processes and states of consciousness. On the morbid side, there is also no end of religious pathology; "cults," "Jonestown," and "Moonies" have become household terms.

Small wonder then that the study of religion, in any of its forms, has assumed new importance for both psychology and sociology. Sociologists have been particularly active in studying "the new religions" and in attempting to connect their emergence with larger social patterns and possible pathologies. They have therefore tended to link religious motivation to inadequacies at the social level, and immaturities at the psychological. And of course they are often correct since there is no shortage of evidence that religious immaturity and pathology reflect their psychological counterparts.

And yet the nagging question remains, Could we be missing something? Is this really all there is to religion? After all, the great saints and sages, Buddha, Christ, Lao Tzu, Shankara, Aurobindo, and others have been said to represent some of the highest levels of human development and to have had the greatest impact on human history. So at least said Toynbee, Tolstoy, Bergson, James, Schopenhauer, Nietzsche, and Maslow, among others. Thus we may ask, Are our guiding sociological assumptions, theories, and methodologies adequate to identify not just immaturity and pathology but also the heights of human experience and development that certain of the great religions claim are both possible and achievable through training?

It is the goal of this book to ensure that these heights are indeed identifiable, and it takes its psychological framework from recent developments in what has come to be known as transpersonal psychology.

The last two decades of psychological research have seen a dramatic surge of interest in areas such as the nature of consciousness and consciousness-modifying technologies, self-regulation of psychophysiological processes, and nonWestern psychologies. The general trend has been toward the recognition that there exist states of consciousness, levels of psychological maturity, and degrees of voluntary control beyond those formerly thought to define the human potential. Humanistic psychology first emerged in an effort to focus attention on these areas; transpersonal psychology followed when even the humanistic model proved inadequate to encompass the full range of phenomena being studied. The term "transpersonal" was chosen to encompass those experiences and states in which the sense of awareness and identity apparently went beyond *(trans)* traditional personality and ego.

In the West they were commonly called peak experiences and were initially assumed to occur only rarely and involuntarily. However, certain Eastern psychologies and religious disciplines were subsequently found to contain not only detailed descriptions of such states but also instructions and technologies for attaining them at will. Suddenly, and with no small surprise to Western psychologists, it began to become apparent that the esoteric core of certain of the great religions, Eastern and Western, which had formerly seemed nonsensical or even pathological, could be understood as technologies for the voluntary control of psychological processes and consciousness. To take but one specific example, meditation could now be seen as an attentional training strategy rather than as a regressive and autistic escape from the world, and this new interpretation now has significant support from empirical research.

Thus it was not that the great religions were necessarily pathological but rather that, prior to an understanding of the nature of such phenomena as state dependency, our own Western psychological framework had not been readily able to encompass such phenomena.

Of course this is not to say that all things Eastern or religious are of this ilk. There are clearly distortions, dogma, pathology, misunderstanding, and misuse around all religions. Indeed, the pragmatic core of rigorous mental training is often buried under exoteric trappings and dogma, or else reserved as an esoteric core for the few deemed able to meet its exacting demands. But where this core of mental training is found, it tends to display marked similarities among apparently quite diverse systems and to point to common psychological principles, worldviews, and transcendental states: the so-called "transcendent unity of religions," "perennial philosophy," and "perennial psychology."

The addition of a transpersonal dimension to traditional psychological models has thus allowed the meaningful reinterpretation of a major sphere of human activity. However, sociological theory has tended to lack a corresponding dimension and has thus sometimes been susceptible to an overly reductionistic approach in its studies of religion. This book therefore aims at adding a transpersonal dimension to sociological theory.

No one is more qualified to do this than Ken Wilber, who is recognized as the preeminent theoretician of transpersonal psychology. In his numerous books and papers he has provided an unparalleled integration of the world's major psychological and religious systems. In *The*

Spectrum of Consciousness he suggested that the apparent conflict between different psychological and religious systems could be resolved by seeing them as addressing different and partly complementary structures of consciousness and levels of the unconscious. In *The Atman Project* he suggested a model for developmental psychology that extended through not only childhood and adolescence but also the various levels of enlightenment. In *Up from Eden* he applied this model to human evolution at large.

Now in *A Sociable God* he takes this same model and uses it as a developmental framework against which the various levels of social interaction can be assessed. This therefore provides a corrective addition to current methods of sociological analysis such as phenomenological-hermeneutics that have lacked critical criteria for hierarchical evaluation. It also provides a means for avoiding the trap of taking one level of social interaction and making it paradigmatic for all. For example, Marx interpreted all behavior in terms of economics, and Freud in terms of sexuality. Art, philosophy, religion, and all "higher" activities thus became expressions of economic oppression or sexual repression.

To this developmental framework Wilber also adds an analysis of the various epistemological modes, the ways in which we obtain knowledge. The fact that sensory, intellectual, and contemplative modes yield different realms or categories of knowledge that are not wholly equivalent or reducible one to another is often forgotten. Conceptual symbolic knowledge cannot wholly be reduced to the objective sensory dimension, nor the contemplative to the conceptual, without resulting in what is called category error. Thus the method for establishing the validity of each realm's knowledge is specific: analytic-empirical for objective data, hermeneutics for symbolic communication, and direct gnostic apprehension for the contemplative.

After delineating these general schemata, Wilber then applies them to specific, especially religious, issues confronting sociology today. First he performs the much-needed task of differentiating among the many and varied ways in which the term "religion" has been used, suggesting that much current confusion stems from imprecise or even mixed usage.

Next he turns to the evolution of religion and interprets its current status and directions against his developmental framework. Our current progression away from mythic belief toward increasing rationalization has been widely interpreted as evidence of an anti- or post-religious evolution. But Wilber reframes this whole movement by noting that this type of progression is an appropriate phase-specific shift as the prerational yields to the rational *on its way to the transrational*. From this evolutionary perspective our current phase is seen as anti-religious only if religion is equated, as it often is, with the prerational rather than with any of several levels on the prerational–rational–transrational developmental hierarchy. This remarkable perspective also allows a method of determining what Wilber calls the authenticity of a religion: the degree to which it fosters development to the transrational levels. This he differentiates from "legitimacy," which he defines as the degree to which a religion fills the psychological and social needs of a population at its current developmental level. And all this leads directly to one of the more seminal parts of the book.

The current religious ferments and the new religions can be examined precisely in light of their responses to the current developmental phase of increasing rationality. Wilber suggests that three major types of sociological responses are now occurring: first, attempting to cling to the now outmoded mythic levels (e.g., "moral majority"); second, embracing the ongoing rational-secularization process (such as the liberal intelligentsia tend to do); and third, in a minority of cases, attempting actual transrational transformation, not by denying rationality but by embracing it *and* going beyond it via intensive yogic-gnostic practice. It is this latter group that Wilber suggests may provide effective catalysts for a broader-scale evolutionary advance, if indeed such is to occur. The importance of such widespread maturation to full development of the rational level, and then beyond, is difficult to overestimate. Our willingness and ability to correct the vast amounts of worldwide suffering from preventable causes such as malnutrition, poverty, overpopulation, sociogenic pathology, and oppression, as well as to avoid massive, if not total, self-destruction, may depend on it. The importance of Ken Wilber's contribution of a testable, critical, comprehensive, sociological model capable of guiding assessments of these evolutionary shifts is likewise not to be underestimated.

This could have been a very lengthy book. The number of novel ideas and suggested syntheses it contains within its few pages is remarkable. The author has chosen to give us an heuristic framework rather than a detailed text. Nonetheless, this outline may well be sufficient to keep both sociologists and psychologists busy researching and filling it out for many years to come, for it has suggested a way to move the psychology and sociology of religion to a new watershed.

ROGER WALSH, M.D., PH.D.

Editor's Note

A Sociable God was first published by McGraw-Hill in 1983 with the subtitle *A Brief Introduction to a Transcendental Sociology*. Shambhala Publications reissued the book in 1984 with it current subtitle, *Toward a New Understanding of Religion*. The 2005 edition is based on the slightly corrected text that appears in *The Collected Works of Ken Wilber*, vol. 3 (Boston: Shambhala Publications, 1999).

A SOCIABLE GOD

Introduction to the 2005 Edition

METHODOLOGICAL OUTLAW
My Life as a Dishwasher

A SOCIABLE GOD is still one of my favorite books. Its central points, I am happy to report, are as valid today as they were when the book was first published. In fact, I am even happier to report, I believe its essential message is even more important, more valid, than ever. For what has happened in the two decades since its first release—when it was attacked from virtually all sides, including both the dominant academic culture (of deconstructive postmodernism) and the dominant counter-culture (of Romantic ecoprimitivism)—is that both of those dominant modes of discourse have run their dominating course, and the way is now open to a more integral, balanced, and comprehensive approach to sociology, including the sociology of spiritual engagement. *A Sociable God*, I believe, will stand as a clarion call for *a sociology of depth*, as well as a radically new way to look at religion itself.

The book makes three essential points. One, there are at least *a dozen different meanings of "religious" or "spiritual,"* and we need to take these different meanings into account if our discussions of those topics are to make any sense at all. Most conversations about religion and spirituality proceed as if those words were transparent, whereas they are anything but. At the very least, there is a profound difference between a spirituality that helps one translate and a spirituality that helps one transform. Some types of religion obfuscate, some oppress, some liber-ate. At any given moment, which function of religion are we discussing?

Two, there are of degrees of authenticity in various religious and

I

spiritual engagements, and further, *a way to adjudicate or judge those degrees of depth*. There are, for example, important differences between prerational spirituality and postrational spirituality. Likewise, there are important differences between *legitimacy* (or how well a spiritual movement facilitates *translation*) and *authenticity* (or how well it facilitates *transformation*). Further—and this is a crucial point of the book—there are valid ways that a religious movement can judge its own degree of depth according to standards that would be acceptable to those within the movement itself. These ways involve developmental unfolding of the religion's own values, according to reports from within the hermeneutic circle of the religion itself. Thus, the idea that "better" or "worse" cannot be applied to religious or spiritual engagements is simply not true. This is a radically new approach to adjudicating or judging the degree of depth of any spiritual movement, an approach that involves developmental holism (as carefully outlined in the following pages).[1]

Three, a more balanced and comprehensive approach to religion and spirituality would take all of those factors into account, thus allowing us to situate spirituality more adequately in the modern and postmodern world. *A Sociable God* was the first book to call for a vertical dimension of depth to be added to our study of interior realities in general, and particularly our sociology of religious and spiritual engagements. I personally believe that this point alone renders this book as important as any on the subject.

A few years ago, Shambhala Publications/Random House brought out my *Collected Works*. Going through that material, I was struck to find that, with only a few early exceptions, the essential points in the twenty-five or so books I had written were still valid; research continued to support their major conclusions and often supported them even more. I was curious about why, other than dumb good luck, that was so. It finally dawned on me: it was the methodology that I had adopted in even the earliest books, a methodology I would come to call *integral methodological pluralism* and summarize in the phrase "Everybody is right."

"Everybody is right" means that, when it comes to the quest for the Good, the True, and the Beautiful, no human mind is capable of producing one hundred percent error. Thus, *everybody* has some important, if partial, truths to offer, and the knowledge quest is therefore not about "who is right and who is wrong," but rather finding a way that all of the various truths can fit together.

When it comes to a method for doing so, the result is integral methodological pluralism, which means that we allow (and rely on) every major mode of acquiring experience—every major methodology, paradigm, injunction, exemplar, technique, and so on—because each of them, without exception, is delivering some important piece of the overall puzzle. Where so many other scholars spent their time picking one or two methodologies and condemning all the others, I was busy weaving them all together.

As I look at the main points I just outlined that are found in *A Sociable God*, I am struck again by how those points depend upon an integral methodological pluralism, a holistic inclusion of all of the major different approaches to the topic of spirituality. And I am equally struck by how radical that approach still is. Academia, as elsewhere, is still a battleground of competing paradigms, turf wars, us-versus-them mentality, first-tier partialities, and civil-war casualties strewn on the landscape like so many corpses at an academic Gettysburg. Somehow this is supposed to advance our self-understanding.

It also dawned on me why I had preferred to be a dishwasher for a decade instead of teach in academia. I was a methodological outlaw in the very inclusiveness of the methodology itself. My approach was outlawed in both cultural and countercultural academies, not because it was partial, but because it was radically holistic. I included those things that shouldn't be included, I embraced those methodologies that were pox-ridden for the orthodox, I loved those injunctions despised by those in power, I reached out to those experiences on the margin and beyond. In including all sides of the argument, I was disowned by all sides.

The holistic truth and I went our lonely way. And yet, today, all of that has begun to change, at least a little bit, as the smoking ruins over the battlefields of partiality have left academia more than a little shellshocked. Integral methodological pluralism, because it includes the most amount of truth from the most number of sources based on the most amount of evidence in the most holistic fashion possible, is here to stay in its broad outlines, and for the simple reason that it honors and includes more truth than any of the alternatives. This is why the essential points in *A Sociable God* are still relevant today. They were originally advanced by including truths that were marginalized at the time—such as developmental holarchy—but which constitute a crucial piece of the overall puzzle. By including those truths then, as now, a much more accurate—and certainly enduring—picture of religion and spirituality emerges.

At the end of this preface I will return to my life as a methodological outlaw and make a few closing remarks on integral methodological pluralism. First, allow me to elaborate a little bit on the three main points of *A Sociable God*.

WHOSE GOD IS THIS, ANYWAY?

The first is that what we call "religion" or "spirituality" is not a single entity or function or view, but rather, *there are at least a dozen considerably different meanings of the word*, pointing to a dozen different functions of this enormously complex thing we call religion, and, needless to say, none of those functions can be equated (although they almost always are). But all talk of "religion and science" or "religion and spirituality" or "religion and the modern world" is virtually useless until we can specify more precisely just what we mean by the term "religion" or "spirituality." *A Sociable God* discusses nine of these different meanings (e.g., the claim that religious realities are nonrational; that they involve ultimate concern; that they are regressive and infantile, mechanisms of social cohesion, immortality projects, the result of evolutionary factors, defense mechanisms, personal realities that must be approached nonreductionistically—and so on). Which of those definitions is right? All of them, surely, in complex ways, and all of them must be taken into account in the incredibly important discussion of the nature and meaning of religion and spirituality in the modern and postmodern world.

It has recently become commonplace to differentiate "religion" and "spirituality," which is yet another interesting definition. According to this view, "religion" is institutional, rigid, dogmatic, and authoritarian, whereas "spirituality" is alive, vital, experiential, and personal. This judgment, common among Baby Boomer writers, may contain a degree of truth, which I'll return to, but it often tends to obscure more than illumine, because it soon becomes apparent that "spiritual" here simply means a religious truth or experience that is true for me, but if that spiritual truth gets passed on to another person, and certainly if it gets passed on to another generation, then it must by definition become institutionalized. It soon becomes apparent that individuals who use the distinction between "religion" and "spirituality" are pointing to a spiritual truth for themselves, but they haven't given much thought to what happens if they wanted to pass this spiritual experience or truth on to another human being, because as soon as they do so, their "spirituality" starts to look a lot like "religion." In other words, in most cases of how these words are used, "spirituality" is simply religion for me; once my spirituality is shared with another, or passed on to another generation, then I am faced with all the same problems of "religion" that I temporarily avoided by introducing the distinction.

Still, the distinction is indeed widespread, where "spiritual" is usually taken to mean "experiential" and "true for me," and "religion," when opposed to "spirituality," means dogmatic and institutional *beliefs* as opposed to *direct experiences*. Notice, in that regard, that because "religious" is often equated with "mere belief" as opposed to "direct experience," then the hybrid phrase "religious experience" tends to come close to how the word "spiritual" is now often used. When William James wrote about "the varieties of religious experience," he was writing about spiritual experience as the term is used today. He coupled the word "religious" with "experience," which is what "spiritual" usually now means.

Because those definitions are widely used, let me say that this is a book that deals with both religious beliefs and spiritual experiences. In fact, it outlines a spectrum from "belief" to "faith" to "direct experiences" to "permanent realization." This is an important continuum, I feel, and its implications are explored in the following pages. If I occasionally use "religion" and "spirituality" interchangeably, context will determine which is meant.

Point number one is simply that the word "religious" has at least a dozen different meanings hiding out in it, meanings that need to be unpacked and explicitly included in our discussions. This analysis is an endeavor that I have continued right up to today. For example, in *Integral Psychology*, I focus specifically on spiritual experience (or "spirituality") and point out that there are at least five very different meanings involved when people speak of spiritual experiences. All five of those meanings are valid, I believe, but we simply must specify which is meant whenever we make statements about spiritual experience.

For example, for some people, a spiritual experience means having an *altered state*—perhaps a *peak experience* of being one with nature. For others, having a spiritual experience means to possess a certain *attitude* (such as love or compassion). For others, a spiritual experience might involve reaching some of the *higher stages* of meditation practice. For still others, spirituality might involve its own line of development, a particular path or *spiritual intelligence* that one can develop like any other capacity or intelligence. Thus, the way "spirituality" has actually been used by people, it can mean having an altered state of consciousness, or possessing a particular attitude, or reaching a particular stage of development, or being a specific developmental line itself. So: state of consciousness, stage of consciousness, attitude, line, and trait: each has in fact been used by people when they speak of spirituality. Which of those five is correct? Once again, I believe all of them have important moments of truth that should be included in any comprehensive or integral approach to spirituality (and hence also institutional spirituality or religion in general).

Yet, odd as it sounds, I have seen virtually no discussion of spirituality or religion that does so. Just yesterday I saw an essay entitled "The Spiral Dynamics Approach to Religion," and religion was again treated as if it were a single thing, instead of at least a dozen wildly different things. Don't get me wrong, I'm a fan of Spiral Dynamics (a psychosocial developmental model based on the research of Clare Graves), but using it for yet another monolithic description of what "religion" means is much less than helpful. This particular paper had taken one of the dozen or so meanings, functions, dimensions, or aspects of "religion" and equated all religion with that one narrow function, to produce an equally narrow result.

Likewise, it is still quite common to get into endless arguments about whether there are any forms of valid or authentic childhood spirituality. I have seen scholars red-faced and screaming over this issue, hurling epithets at each other in a display barely one notch above a food fight. So polarized is this discussion that simply asking, "Which of a dozen meanings of 'spirituality' are you referring to?" is taken to be dim-witted at best, demonic at worst (although one critic did accuse me of being a dim-witted demon, apparently combining the worst of both hells. Well, I'm integral if nothing else).

But the simple fact is, human beings can have a peak experience or altered state at virtually any stage of development; and thus, if by "spirituality" you mean an altered state, of course children can have authentic peak experiences, but if by "spirituality" you mean postconventional stages of development, then of course they cannot. This might be the end of the discussion, except apparently nobody wants it ended that quickly, since academic food fights are the stuff of manly scholars, one supposes. In any event, demons and dimwits are still at it, wonderfully, each of them pitting their one-twelfth of religion against the other guy's one-twelfth, each calling that the whole.

THREE-DIMENSIONAL FEMINISM

The second major point of this book is that, when focusing on that aspect of religion or spirituality that involves authenticity (or the degree of depth of a spiritual engagement), there is actually a way to discern "better" and "worse" or "higher" and "lower" engagements. This claim, needless to say, has evoked criticisms that made "demonic" and "dim-witted" sound appealing.

Here we stumble onto perhaps the most misunderstood concept in developmental psychology, that of hierarchy. Not only is the concept misunderstood, it is willfully misunderstood. As but one example, take Carol Gilligan's wonderful book, *In a Different Voice*. It is probably the most often quoted book by feminists of any persuasion, and its profoundly distorted conclusions—much like those of Thomas Kuhn's *The Structure of Scientific Revolutions*—are a cautionary tale in the culture wars. Both books were similarly distorted, for similar reasons, by apparently similar motives.[2]

Gilligan's book is usually summarized (misleadingly) as follows: According to Gilligan, men and women think differently. Men think using hierarchies, which involve judgmental ranking; women think nonhierarchically or relationally. Men use *ranking*; women use *linking*. Men reason using a logic of rights, justice, and autonomy; but women reason "in a different voice," using a logic of care, relationship, and responsibility. Since oppression and social inequalities involve ranking and brutal hierarchies, then we need more female linking values in order to establish peace, relational care, partnership societies, and ecological harmony. "Away from all hierarchies!" became the battle cry.

Gilligan did indeed suggest that men tend to think hierarchically and women nonhierarchically. But she went on to point out that both men and women develop through three or four "hierarchical stages" (which is her phrase). That is, women think relationally or nonhierarchically, *but nonhierarchical thinking itself develops through four hierarchical stages.*

These four female hierarchical stages Gilligan called *selfish, care, universal care*, and *integrated*. Her point is that both men and women develop through those four hierarchical stages of moral reasoning, but each of them does so in a different voice: men develop through the moral hierarchy using a logic of rights and justice; women develop through the same moral hierarchy using a logic of care and relationship.

Thus, at stage 1 (*selfish* or *egocentric*), men are selfish in agentic ways, women are selfish in communal ways (using social ostracism to punish others). At stage 2 (*care* or *ethnocentric*), men extend rights to those of their group, tribe, or nation—but demonize those in other ethnic groups—and women extend love and care to their own group or tribe, but gladly offer up sons to the battlefield to slay the enemy. At stage 3 (*universal care* or *worldcentric*), the masculine principle extends rights and justice to all human beings, regardless of race, color, sex, or creed; and the feminine principle extends care and compassion to all humans. Of course, actual men and women are a mixture of masculine and feminine modes, with individuals containing various combinations of both. At stage 4 *(integrated)*, the masculine and feminine principles in each person can be integrated in that person, according to Gilligan, resulting in a union of the contrasexual attitudes in each.

In each stage of a developmental hierarchy, the succeeding stage is indeed part of a "higher-archy," because each succeeding stage has more love, more compassion, more care, more justice, more consciousness, more rights, and so on. Far from being a bad thing, nested hierarchies are the means of reducing prejudice, reducing oppression, reducing "isms" of one sort or another (racism, sexism, speciesism, etc.). The higher one is in a growth higher-archy, the *more care* and the *less oppression* one is inclined to possess, by definition and by factual research.

Most feminists took the first half of what Gilligan said ("Women don't think hierarchically") but ignored the second half ("Women's non-hierarchical thinking develops through four hierarchical stages"). When the battle cry became "Away from all hierarchies!" it actually meant "Away from all growth!"—and thus away from the means of reducing oppression, reducing sexism, reducing racism. In championing nonhierarchy only, these social critics devastated the one means of truly overcoming prejudice, racism, and sexism; they inadvertently championed exactly the attitudes and approaches that fostered and supported ongoing racism, sexism, and ethnocentric prejudice.

Hence the furor surrounding Barbara Ehrenreich's May 2004 *Los Angeles Times* editorial, "Feminism's Assumptions Upended," which was subtitled "A Uterus Is Not a Substitute for a Conscience." Feminism, in promoting nonhierarchy as the feminine mode of being, had actually fallen into a flatland feminism that merely equated "female" with "moral," overlooking the fact that female values at stages 1 and 2 are a malevolent force in today's world. What we need in today's world are fewer female values from stages 1 and 2 (egocentric and ethnocentric) and more male and female values from stages 3 and 4 (worldcentric and integral). Female values from stages 1 and 2 contribute to Auschwitz and Wounded Knee just as much as do male values from stages 1 and 2 (which, in so many words, is Barbara Ehrenreich's main point).

But this is not "feminism's assumptions upended" as much as it is "flatland feminism's assumptions upended," which indeed they are. The reason that "a uterus is not a substitute for a conscience" is that there are, so to speak, four levels of uterine thinking. The sad fact is that, in championing merely "female values" instead of hierarchical female values, depth was erased from the feminist equation. By focusing merely on any type of "relational linking" as *the* female value, the net result was often a regressive feminine value system, which inadvertently took women from worldcentric care to ethnocentric care to egocentric selfish, a move that was meant to heal the nation, heal the world, heal the planet.

Alas, the cure offered was part of the disease. In denouncing all hierarchies, feminists effectively aborted the means of their own growth and development, a miscarriage revealed in their own misanthropy. Instead of realizing that there are at least four levels of uterine thinking (or four levels of relational thinking), they simply championed "the feminine mode of being," or claimed that linking plus ranking equaled partnership societies. But ethnocentric females supported Nazism just as stridently as their husbands and sons did. Ethnocentric white females in the American South today support the KKK just as much as their white male cousins do. Those ethnocentric females are indeed involved in linking and relationship, but it is a linking that extends only to the edge of their tribe, their kin, their clan—the Ku Klux Klan, in this case.

In short, flatland feminism focused only on the linking and relating, and forgot to notice that there are at least four levels of relating, four levels of linking, from the most brutal and barbaric to the most inclusive and sublime. Simply championing the "feminine mode of being" could in fact be contributing to the worst barbarisms imaginable, if those female values are stage-1 or stage-2 in Carol Gilligan's model. This world does not need more female or relational or linking values; it needs more stage-3 and stage-4 female values, and a lot less female values from stage-1 and stage-2, which will be the death of us all if left to their own devices. That is exactly why "a uterus is not a substitute for a conscience." The fact that such a simple, obvious statement could cause such an uproar shows how deeply embedded the flatland mentality still is.

On the other hand, the introduction of deep feminism—along with deep spirituality—at least gives us a chance to add a dimension of depth, growth, development, evolutionary unfolding, and genuinely vertical transformation—from selfish to care to universal care to integrated. *Which level will our female, linking, relational values stem from?* Shall I relate only to myself (and not care for others), only to my tribe (and hate all other tribes), only to all humans (and hence stop at speciesism), or to all sentient beings (and hence stop at God)?

Such a "three-dimensional feminism" is exactly what *A Sociable God* attempted to offer.[3] And now, some two decades into the wasteland created by flatland social criticism, flatland feminism, and flatland spirituality, the world is in a place where I believe it can begin to hear this message and start to introduce a dimension of vertical depth into our social agendas. Such an *integral feminism*—a three-dimensional feminism, as well as three-dimensional sociology, ecology, spirituality, psychology, etc.—is being pursued at Integral Institute, and if this more inclusive and comprehensive approach appeals to you, please see the last few paragraphs in this preface for ways you can join us in this enriching endeavor.

MY GOD IS BETTER THAN YOUR GOD

But, indeed, how can we be sure that in making judgments like "Worldcentric is better than ethnocentric," we are morally justified? However high-minded it sounds, how can we be sure?

This is one of the profoundly useful aspects of developmental studies. The entire point of developmental research is that, when done correctly, the researchers themselves are not imposing their own value systems on their subjects but are simply drawing out, in a noninvasive and hermeneutic fashion, the unfolding of a group's own values.

Typical developmentalists work as follows. They might pose a particular question or dilemma to a group of people. Gilligan, for example, asked a group of women if a woman has a right to an abortion. The researchers note the responses and see if they fall into any patterns. Gilligan, for example, found that the women's responses tended to fall into three (and later, four) categories (selfish, care, universal care, integrated). Developmentalists then follow these responses over time, often long periods of time (years or even decades), and see if individuals change their responses. Researchers might find, for example, that if a woman gives the "care" response, a few years later she might give the "universal care" response, but not the "selfish" response. That is, the developmentalists might find that these responses have a *directionality*, that there is a *sequence* involved—in other words, these responses are *stages* in a *developmental* sequence, which is what Gilligan found. Her four responses were actually four stages in a hierarchical developmental unfolding.

We saw that in such a hierarchy of increasing care and consciousness, each higher stage is indeed higher, meaning that it has a greater capacity for care, concern, relationship, and consciousness. But "higher" according to whom? *According to those giving the responses themselves.* In other words, any genuine developmental sequence is not a meta-narrative imposed on the subjects by an outsider, but is pronounced on the sequence from within, by the subjects themselves, as they reflect on their own responses. Those who give the universal-care response claim that it is wider, deeper, truer than the care response that they once offered. Thus, the judgment that this sequence is a value sequence—that higher stages are better—comes from those going through the stages themselves, from those who have experienced the different responses themselves, and not from some outside "authority" or "hegemonic imperialist" or "patriarchal" researcher. A concerned, hermeneutic, judgment from within: this is the essence of developmentalism done well.

GENEALOGY: WHAT IT MEANS TO GROW

Such a concerned genealogy (or hermeneutic developmentalism) is one of the great contributions of constructive postmodernism. As explained in "Who Ate Captain Cook?" (Sidebar A to *Boomeritis*, posted at http://wilber.shambhala.com), there are two major paths through postmodern pluralism. One is *pluralistic relativism,* and one is *genealogy* (or developmentalism). The integral approach takes the important insights of both and weaves them together with other essential methodologies to give us a multiplex of perspectives, each important, none of which can be ignored.

But, alas, the developmental approach has indeed been ignored, marginalized, repressed, and outlawed from the dominant discourse of academic postmodernity. The result, as we were saying, has been a flatland sociology, flatland feminism, flatland ecology, flatland spirituality, flatland humanities, all parading under the guise of social equality and freedom, all in fact sadly oppressing depth and care and consciousness, and doing so inadvertently because the only demonstrable way of increasing freedom, care, and social concern—namely, by developing through the nested hierarchy of increasing compassion—has been pronounced anathema and scrubbed from the postmodernist agenda. That has, perhaps, been the saddest irony of the past two or three decades—that those who wanted most to end social oppression actually ended the one means of achieving their goals, namely, hierarchical growth through the nested spheres of increasing care and consciousness.

A dimension of depth is what allows one to move from pluralism to genealogy. Both attempt to navigate the plethora of interpretations that postmodernity has irrevocably handed us. Both agree that there is no single pre-given world, no single interpretation of reality that can compel rational consensus, no single value system that argument can convincingly support. The postmodern world is a pluralistic world, a world of ineradicable diversity, multiculturalism, multiple value systems, unavoidably.

But genealogy goes one step further to transcend and include pluralism. It takes any particular response a person might give in this pluralistic world and follows that response over time. Genealogy is pluralism plus history. It traces any response from its birth across an arc of time. This is why the word part *gen*—from the Greek meaning "born," as in *genealogy, genesis,* and *genetic* epistemology—is often found in the terminology of developmental studies. Genealogy in its most sophisticated and careful form is developmentalism, quite like what Carol Gilligan did—or Clare Graves, Jane Loevinger, Susanne Cook-Greuter, Robert Kegan, and so on.

Some changes in responses seem to be abrupt ruptures, with no obvious cause or relation to their predecessors. But most changes are clearly related to their predecessors in at least a few discernible ways. In Gilligan's nested hierarchy, for example, each succeeding response takes more perspectives into account (selfish is merely a first-person perspective; *care* involves adding a second-person perspective; *universal care* involves adding a third-person perspective, and so on). Within those genealogical streams, we saw that there is a value current or *directionality* clearly discernible and clearly announced by those who themselves are traversing those currents: worldcentric care is *better* than ethnocentric care, which is *better* than egocentric selfish.

To the extent that spiritual engagements involve care and consideration for others—and a capacity to take into account perspectives other than one's own egoic perspective—then to that extent as well, some spiritual engagements are better, truer, deeper, more authentic than others. This vertical dimension of depth means that there are degrees of authenticity in spiritual engagements (as judged by those making that particular journey and who have experienced it from within, and not merely as an exterior judgment according to some privileged meta-narrative). The God of my maturity is better than the God of my immaturity.

And that "better" turns out to have stunning similarities across belief systems and across social groups.[4] For example, in any group (East or West, North or South), those who have experienced *both* a worldcentric perspective *and* an ethnocentric perspective *within their own group* claim that the former response is better, higher, deeper. At no point does genealogy claim that, for example, a stage in my culture is better than a stage in some other culture, but only that a stage in any culture can be judged better or worse by those in that culture themselves, and is only valid as a stage-conception if it springs from within. It is simply that, in any culture where we find a sequence such as egocentric to ethnocentric to worldcentric, those going through that sequence as it appears in that culture assert that worldcentric is better than ethnocentric, and to that extent is similar to other cultures (and hence is a cross-cultural similarity).

A Sociable God was the first book to explore this dimension of depth as it applies to cross-cultural spiritual engagements. In doing so it introduced a sociology of depth, including a three-dimensional feminism and an approach to religion and spirituality that recognizes a vertical dimension of increasing care and consciousness.

THE PRE/POST FALLACY

The idea that there is a vertical dimension of depth, of developmental depth, in religious and spiritual unfolding, is actually quite similar to Gilligan's four stages of female hierarchy: selfish, care, universal care, and integrated. *A Sociable God* uses a more sophisticated genealogy of archaic, magic, mythic, rational, psychic, subtle, and causal—but those are all variations on the general theme, and scales such as Gilligan's are included in comprehensive overviews such as that offered in *Integral Psychology*.

Another version of the notion of degrees of depth is found in the idea of the *pre/post fallacy*, which I introduced right around the time that *A Sociable God* was written. Perhaps no other idea of mine has caused such turmoil, so perhaps I should say a few words about it.

The general idea is simple enough: there are important differences between spiritual experiences that are *pre*-rational and those that are *post*-rational, and yet people are always confusing them. Starting with me: I discovered the pre/post fallacy by looking at my own mistakes: by looking, that is, at why the Romantic viewpoint seems at first to make so much sense, why almost everybody seems to start their study of spirituality with a Romantic viewpoint, and yet it cannot handle the actual data and evidence of phylogenetic and ontogenetic development.

The general Romantic view is fairly straightforward: infants, and dawn humans, start out immersed in an unconscious union with the world at large (and with the pure Self or pure Spirit)—peacefully embedded in a type of primal paradise (either a literal earthly Eden, a foraging ecological wisdom, or an infant fusion "with the mother and the world in bliss"). Through subsequent development, this primal paradise is lost as the rational-ego emerges from this primal Ground, breaks and fragments this "nondissociated" state, and creates thereby a world of sin, suffering, ecological catastrophe, patriarchal brutality, and general malevolence. But the self (and humanity) can drop its overly analytic, divisive, and fragmented stance by returning to, *and recapturing*, the wholeness of the original embeddedness (but now in a mature and conscious form). The original wholeness, now combined with analytic capacities, will result in a renewed heaven-on-earth, ecologically sound and balanced, and usher in a liberated nondissociated consciousness, which is enlightened and spiritual in the deepest and truest sense.

As I explained in the introduction to volume 2 of the *Collected Works*, I started writing both *The Atman Project* and *Up from Eden* in order to prove this Romantic conception. If nothing else, it cannot be said that I do not understand that view or that I have never had any sympathy for it. I was, in my earlier years, its most ardent fan. But the more I tried to make the Romantic orientation explain the actual evidence, the more dismally it failed. During a long period of intellectual anguish, I slowly abandoned a strictly Romantic stance (while keeping some of its more durable truths), and moved to adopt the only view that seemed to me to be able to genuinely handle the great preponderance of evidence—and that was the developmental or evolutionary model.

In tracing out my early, fervent embrace of Romanticism, I was able to reconstruct what I believe are the intellectual errors that led to that embrace—and they are all summarized by the pre/post (or pre/trans) fallacy. The pre/post fallacy simply says: in any recognized developmental sequence, where development proceeds from pre-X to X to post-X, the pre states and the post states, because they are both non-X states, tend to be confused and equated, simply because they appear, at first glance, to be so similar. Prerational and postrational are both nonrational; preconventional and postconventional are both nonconventional; prepersonal and transpersonal are both nonpersonal; preverbal and transverbal are both nonverbal, and so on.

Once we confuse pre and post, then one of two unfortunate things tends to happen: we either reduce postconventional, transrational, superconscious states to prerational, infantile, oceanic fusion (as did Freud) or we elevate infantile, childish, prerational states to transcendental, transrational, transpersonal glory (as the Romantics often did). We reduce post to pre, or we elevate pre to post. *Reductionism* is well understood; *elevationism* was the great province of the Romantics.

Despite what seems to be the emotional appeal of Romanticism, the overwhelming preponderance of evidence points to the fact that infants (and early hominids) did not exist in a postrational heaven but in a prerational slumber. The awakening of the rational, self-conscious ego out of this prerational, prereflexive slumber did indeed involve a painful awakening to the horrors of the manifest world, but that awakening was not a fall from a previous superconscious state, but the growth up and out of a subconscious immersion. The subconscious immersion is *already* fallen—it *already* exists in the manifest world of hunger, pain, finitude, and mortality—it just hasn't the awareness to fully register those painful facts. Likewise, the rational-ego, far from being the height of ontological alienation, is actually halfway through the growth to superconscious awakening. The ego isn't actually in the lowest hell, it just feels like it.

But the Romantics, *correctly* realizing that Spirit is beyond mere rationality, and *correctly* realizing that the rational-ego stands outside of, and even resists, nondual spiritual consciousness, then made the classic *elevationist* fallacy: they assumed the prehistorical slumber in Paradise was the primal whole out of which humanity fell, and back to which humanity must return, in order to usher in a transrational heaven. And that deeply *regressive* view of human potentials would set the stage for all of the well-known downsides, even horrors, of Romanticism: an obsession with self and self-feelings (regressing from worldcentric to ethnocentric to egocentric), hedonistic amorality (regressing from postconventional/universal care to ethnocentric/conventional care to preconventional/selfish)—all of which claimed to be "beyond reason," whereas most of it was simply beneath it.

All of that became obvious as I reconstructed my own mistakes, and all of that I worked out in the concept of the pre/post fallacy. The idea itself was initially presented in *The Atman Project* (1978) and was worked out in detail in the essay "The Pre/Trans Fallacy," which was included in the book *Eye to Eye* (appearing in volume 3 of the *Collected Works* along with *A Sociable God*), which shows that this idea was still very clearly etched in my mind as I was writing *A Sociable God*; and a good thing, too, in my opinion, because it was one of the crucial concepts that allowed the reintroduction of a vertical depth dimension into an intellectual landscape that was rapidly going flatland in both the conventional academic culture and, more sadly, in the counterculture as well (represented by institutions from Naropa University to the California Institute of Integral Studies), which should have known better but did not, proudly.

In the twenty years since its publication, two types of criticism have been leveled at the pre/post fallacy. The reductionists attack it for allowing the existence of *any* postconventional, transrational, transpersonal states (they are still ever so busy reducing all trans states to sneaky insurrections of infantile, prerational silliness). And elevationists indignantly attack it, often vitriolically, for supposedly claiming that infants and children (and dawn humans) are only prerational, without access to any sort of spiritual or transpersonal states. Both of these attacks are what one would expect if the pre/post fallacy were true; still, both sides have presented my view as much more rigid than it ever was.

First, with the reductionists, I do not think that all, or even most, of those states that claim to be transpersonal, postrational, or spiritual are actually that. The human capacity for self-delusion is too enormous to take all such claims at face value. A highly critical, occasionally skeptical, and sometimes even polemical attitude must be our constant companion on the road to any sort of truth. The commodity most lacking in spiritual circles seems to be, indeed, a healthy skepticism, possibly because skepticism is confused with lack of faith, a stance which, if understandable, is deeply misguided. Nonetheless, against the reductionists, I—and a colossal amount of cross-cultural evidence—refuse to dismiss all transpersonal, transrational, mystical states as if they were only irritating irruptions from an infantile primordial slime.

With the elevationists, I can agree, to a point, that various types of spiritual or transpersonal states are available to infants and dawn humans, and I have never denied that. I will first address infants, then the earlier stages of human evolution.

Not in Entire Forgetfulness Do We Come . . .

Let us assume, for the moment, that there actually exist spiritual realities, actual spiritual realities to which we can have genuine access. If we make that assumption, then the available evidence suggests that there are at least two major types of spiritual access in infants and young children. The first is quite controversial, so I will mention it in passing. It involves what I have called "trailing clouds of glory," which refers to all the deeper psychic (or soul) awareness that the individual might bring to this life and that would therefore be present in some sense from conception forward. You might wish to interpret this as actual reincarnation; but it can also be interpreted simply as one's own deepest potentials that are present from the start. I'll pursue this possibility in an endnote.[5]

The second possible type of spiritual experience or awareness to which infants and young children might have access is less controversial, at least if one believes in authentic spiritual experience in the first place. This involves the idea of *states* of consciousness, which are different from *stages* of consciousness. Stages, like those investigated by Carol Gilligan, do indeed emerge in a sequential unfolding and flowering; and, just as you do not find flowers appearing before buds, you do not find postconventional responses occurring before conventional responses and preconventional responses. The evidence is overwhelmingly clear on that particular issue. If we are looking at stages of development, then infancy and childhood rarely if ever contain postconventional responses.

But developmental stages and streams, such as Gilligan's, important as they are, do not exhaust the psyche's inventory. As we were saying, in addition to *stages of consciousness*, there are *states of consciousness*. The most common states of consciousness are waking, dreaming, and deep sleep. For various complicated reasons, the great wisdom traditions often equate those states respectively with body, soul, and spirit. That is: the waking, gross realm of matter (and the body); the dreaming, subtle realm of archetypal images and luminosity (of mind and soul); and the formless, deep causal realm of vast emptiness and pure infinite openness (of spirit). Hence, waking, dream, and deep-sleep states are often correlated with body, soul, and spirit.

Whatever one may think of those correlations, one thing is undeniable: even an infant wakes, dreams, and sleeps. Accordingly, if I maintain that the waking state has access to the material body, and the dreaming state has a type of access to soul, and deep imageless sleep has a type of access to formless spirit, then I should maintain that the infant has some sort of access to body, soul, and spirit, and can experience those spiritual dimensions in some fashion.

I believe there is merit to that argument; it is also a subset of what developmentalists often see in any event—namely, that the self at virtually any *stage* of consciousness or development (e.g., selfish, care, universal care, integrated), can have an altered state or peak experience of some of the major *states* of consciousness (e.g., gross, subtle, causal). Hence, you can actually map states against stages.

For example, using those two simple scales (of four stages and three states), we would have twelve major types of religious or spiritual experiences. The actual content of these experiences would be extremely fluid (and intimately depend upon social and cultural factors as well—what I would later call the quadrants), but the types themselves would be easily recognizable. *A Sociable God* was the first book to introduce such a grid or matrix of spiritual experience, focusing on both the origin of the experience (what realm, dimension, or state is being experienced?) as well as the structure or stage that receives or interprets the experience (is the person's experience of the subtle dream state interpreted through the selfish, care, universal care, or integrated stage?).[6] Thus, a person might indeed have a gross, subtle, causal, or nondual experience, but it will be interpreted—and can only be interpreted—with the mental apparatus that one has available (i.e., that is present at the particular stage of their own development, whether that is selfish, care, universal care, or integrated).

A few years later, Allan L. Combs, coming at the problem from a different angle, would hit upon an essentially similar formulation regarding states and stages and the fact that they can be mapped onto each other, and when we both discovered the basic similarity of our models, we agreed to call this the Wilber-Combs matrix. We have since joined hands as colleagues and considerably refined and sophisticated this matrix, but it remains what I believe is an incredibly useful interpretive analytic for religious and spiritual experiences.

So, does the infant have access to spiritual realities? (And further, does the infant have access to spiritual realities that are necessarily lost by *all* adults and regained by *all* enlightened people?—which is the actual core of the Romantic claim.) Well, the answer depends on what you mean by "spiritual," as we were saying. If we go through the list of, say, the five major meanings of the word "spiritual" given in *Integral Psychology*, we can ask that question of each of those five definitions, which gives us a much more precise and focused set of answers. I have done exactly that in several articles and essays. See, for example, chapter 6, "The Recaptured God," in *The Eye of Spirit*; chapter 11, "Is There a Childhood Spirituality?" in *Integral Psychology*; and "Childhood Spirituality," Excerpt D, http://wilber.shambhala.com.

"Childhood Spirituality" gives a series of examples of authentic childhood spiritual experiences, rooted in peak experiences of the waking, dreaming, deep-sleep, and nondual-flow states that are ever-present in humans to some degree from about four months forward after conception. If there are any similarities in the subtle-dream state of, say, a three-year old and an adult, then the three-year old can have authentic subtle-realm experiences, obviously. But the evidence continues to show that those experiences in the infant and young child are all interpreted through preconventional structures and stages.

The bottom line is that in no sense is the strictly Romantic view correct, because that view gives a very partial slice of the overall picture of the infantile psyche. It seems to contain a series of partial truths, as well as a series of what appear to be serious confusions. What we are faced with, for example, is a four-month-old infant. It spends most of its time crying and screaming, red-faced, agitated, a bundle of impulses and discharges, lacking muscular coordination. Is that a state of *perfect oneness with Ground*? And further, is that the same state that will be *recaptured* upon enlightenment? (Do you really want to recapture that state?) Yet, according to the Romantic view, the infant is completely one with the Ground of Being, in a blissful, nondual, supremely peaceful state of "oneness with the world in bliss and love." Is that true?

In not a single way that I can find is that strictly true. The Romantic conception focuses on something happening in a small slice of the psyche, and equates a type of very limited fusion state with the Ground of All Being, which seems a considerable distortion of a much more complete picture.

Incidentally, every time I mention this idea of an infant being in a state of blissful oneness with the world (and the dynamic ground) to a woman, and especially to a mother, they always look at me like I'm nuts. "Have you ever actually seen a four-month-old infant?" they always ask. The fact is, the only theorists who have ever seriously proposed the idea that the infantile self is perfectly one with the Ground are male academic theorists. It fits a certain abstract, male, categorizing intellectual scheme about being one with Ground, splitting from Ground, reuniting with Ground, etc. Boy gets girl, boy loses girl, boy regains girl.

In any event, if we do indeed focus our attention individually on the five or so common meanings of "spiritual," then we get a different answer to the question each time, and this much more complete (and complicated) response is surely closer to the real situation than simple abstract schemes of oneness, alienation, return to oneness. For example, if we focus on two of the most important meanings of spiritual that we have been discussing—states and stages—then it can be said with a fair amount of confidence that the infantile self does *not* have access to conventional or postconventional or nondual stages, but it *does* have various types of access to many states of consciousness, including the broad states of gross/waking, subtle/dreaming, and causal/sleeping. There is a sense in which, during infancy, poorly differentiated boundaries allow a type of flooding and fusion of gross, subtle, and causal *states*. But again, this is a dreamlike immersion in realms that, when interpreted, are interpreted through childhood narcissism, through Gilligan's egocentric selfish stage, which, in its total contours, few would picture as spiritual in any deep sense.[7]

But in no sense is there a single Ground that is present in the infantile self, broken in the adult self, and then fully regained in the enlightened state—that's just too much of an abstraction (which is only the beginning of the problems with that view, because any careful reading of the properties of "the Ground" that are supposed to be present in the infantile self shows that these are not actually present in the enlightened state. For example, the infant is not one with nirvikalpa samadhi, the infant does not possess the union of nirvikalpa and form known as sahaj, the infant does not possess constant unity consciousness, and so on; not a single actual property of the enlightened state can be found in the infantile self and not found in the adult self. Again, the idea of a complete oneness, necessarily broken, then completely recaptured, is an abstract academic scheme that has little relation to the fluid richness and complexity of the first years of life).

So we cannot claim that the infantile self, in its totality, is one with the Ground of Being in any authentic sense, because parts of its psyche are already limited, fragmented, undeveloped, chaotic, discordant, and much less than unified (as mothers are always reminding us). But because the young self does have genuine access to various gross, subtle, and casual states and experiences (even if they will be interpreted in less than worldcentric ways), the claim that infants and young children lack all spiritual access is also much too extreme. The truth, as always, lies in the middle way.

THE TWO FALLS OF HUMANKIND

The basic confusion that I believe the Romantic disposition makes is this: it correctly intuits that there is indeed a Ground of Being (or a nondual Spirit of some sort); it correctly intuits that we (and all things) have all issued forth from this Ground and are ultimately one with this Ground; and it correctly intuits that we have been cut off from an awareness of our oneness with Ground (which the traditions indicate by saying that the ordinary person from birth is living in a fallen state, living in original sin, or living in a world of illusion and samsara). But Romanticism then mislocates and misidentifies the nature of the Fall. It gets everything else very close to right, but due to that one big confusion, it necessarily creates a series of numerous secondary confusions in an attempt to account for the mess created by the first and major misunderstanding: when the Fall?

I have dealt extensively with this problem going all the way back to *Up from Eden.* The essential solution, I believe, is contained in the idea that there are two basic Falls, if you will: a metaphysical fall and a psychological fall.

The *metaphysical fall* represents *the loss of a conscious oneness with Spirit* and a consequent immersion in a world of sin and separation, duality and finitude, maya and mortality. The *psychological fall* represents a *self-reflexive awareness* of that mess, or an awareness that we are living in a fragmented, torn, alienated world that appears to be separate from Spirit.

My dog, for example, is living in a finite and dualistic world, a world of time and suffering and thirst and desire, but he is not painfully or self-reflexively aware of that fact. He lives in a world that the traditions would characterize as fallen; he is living in samsara, in a world of maya, a world of finitude, hunger, pain, and mortality. Now, according to the traditions, my dog is not actually separated from Spirit; he is in fact unconsciously one with Spirit, for the simple reason that Spirit is the Ground of All Being, and so of course my dog is one with Spirit in an unconscious fashion (if he weren't, he would instantly cease to exist). But because he has not awakened to a conscious oneness with Spirit, he is living in a metaphysically fallen world of duality, maya, samsara, finitude, and mortality.

My dog has not, however, suffered the psychological fall, because he does not have enough self-reflexive awareness to worry about it. Of course he is living in samsara; of course he is not living in nirvana (he cannot get into nirvikalpa samadhi, he cannot consciously have a metanoia or conscious redemption and rebirth). No offense to my dog, but he has suffered the metaphysical fall but not yet the psychological fall.

He's fallen, but doesn't know it. Nor worry about it, nor anguish over it. He's metaphysically fallen, but not psychologically fallen.

So when do those two falls occur in humans? The traditions are absolutely unanimous that the metaphysical fall occurs *prior* to biological birth (so that the infant is *already* born in sin, or is *already* living in samsara: the infant is *not* living in nirvana or nirvikalpa samadhi by any stretch of the imagination, and there is not a single tradition that claims it is). There might be trailing clouds of glory, it is true, and several traditions emphasize that, but those clouds are trails of a dimension *that exists prior to biological birth* (such as the bardo realm), and *not* a definition of the infantile self per se. I have found not a single wisdom tradition that believes otherwise.

So unless you are a Buddha, every infant at birth is already living in samsara, is already living in sin, is already finite, mortal, and caressed by the three marks of all existence: suffering, impermanence, and no-self.[8] In other words, and by whatever name, the infant from conception has already suffered *the metaphysical fall* (i.e., it is *already living in samsara* and not any sort of conscious or unconscious nirvana).[9]

But then there is the second Fall, which is a psychological awakening to our metaphysically fallen state. That Fall occurs, I believe, beginning in infancy and early childhood. Enlightenment, liberation, release, metanoia, or salvation occurs when both falls are overcome by the resurrection or regaining of a conscious oneness with Spirit.

The Romantics simply confuse these two Falls.

They accordingly think that when the psychological fall occurs in early childhood, which indeed it does, then somehow that is actually the metaphysical fall, and worse, they often interpret that to mean that in early infancy or childhood we are somehow actually falling away from (or being separated from a union with) the Ground of Being itself, which, if true, would kill us all immediately.[10]

Based on that confusion, the errors multiply rapidly. Precisely because there is indeed a period in early infancy when the psychological fall has not yet occurred, then if you confuse these two Falls, you will think that during that very early period, the infant is innocent of the metaphysical fall as well. But the relative innocence of infancy is not that the infant is immersed in nirvana (or that it has not yet suffered the metaphysical fall), but that it has not yet suffered the psychological fall. It is not living in conscious nirvana, but it has not yet self-reflexively awakened to the horrors of samsara, even though it is drenched in those horrors constantly (it cries, it screams, it suffers, it has hunger, it has rage, it has fear). In confusing these two Falls, a Romantic theorist will be forced to read deeply spiritual and nondual oneness into infantile states that are often marked by utter chaos, fusion, and confusion (as if that is something you'd want to recapture in enlightenment). Welcome to the pre/post fallacy, elevationist style.

THE EVER-PRESENT GROUND

So when did the metaphysical fall occur? I have discussed this at length in *Up from Eden*, *Eye to Eye*, and *The Eye of Spirit* (see especially the last). In essence, we can say that it occurred prior to the Big Bang; or prior to birth through the bardo; or prior to this and every moment in our contracting away from infinity, contracting away from the ever-present and timeless Ground that is the nature and condition of this and every moment. My point (elaborated in those books) is that all three of those are the same metaphysical (or involutionary) fall, which has nothing to do with infancy, and everything to do with our present relation with the Ever-Present Ground.

This is obviously a large and challenging issue, and if you are interested, I suggest you consult *The Eye of Spirit* for an ongoing discussion. In the meantime, I think we can say that the Romantics intuited a deeply enduring truth about being one with Spirit, falling away from that Oneness, and returning to that Oneness. But, being caught in the classic elevationist wing of the pre/trans fallacy, they were forced to attribute enlightened qualities to an infantile self that are, to put it mildly, hard for even a mother to see.

DAWN HUMANS, DAWN SPIRIT

Notice that the pre/post fallacy says that *in any recognized developmental sequence*, pre and post are often confused. It does not say that childhood is nothing but pre. As we just saw, there are types of *transient access to spiritual states* (gross, subtle, and causal) even in the infantile self (because even the infant wakes, dreams, and sleeps). Rather, the pre/trans fallacy is meant to call attention to the extensive types of confusion that occur even in fully recognized developmental sequences. For example, we have been discussing the fact that researchers from Graves to Gilligan agree that moral judgment moves from preconventional to conventional to postconventional modes. The pre/post fallacy simply says that, given this recognized sequence, preconventional and postconventional are often confused, simply because both are nonconventional. And we have to look no further than the general New Age movement to find abundant evidence of preconventional impulse being confused with postconventional liberation; prerational self-absorption being confused with transrational freedom; preverbal hedonism confused with transverbal wisdom. Alas, it is almost always the Romantic orientation, with its sincere but deeply confused elevationism, that drives the entire display, with self-obsession elevated to Self-realization, divine egoism exalted as divine liberation, rampant narcissism paraded as transcendental freedom. But the important nugget of truth contained in the Romantic intuition is that, indeed, we have fallen from a union with Spirit (a union found, not in the dregs of an infantile past, but in the depths of the timeless present), and we can indeed *regain* that spiritual union—but *only* if we grow in a transcendence of ego, and not simply recapture an infantile self.

What, then, of the earlier stages of human development? And not just the dawn state of perhaps a million years ago, but the stages of tribal foraging and village horticulture? Are we arrogantly to pronounce indigenous tribes "inferior"? And are we really to claim they had no access to transrational, transpersonal spirituality? Romantic theorists bristle at the thought that anyone would so callously pronounce whole epochs to be "inferior" or "lacking in genuine spirituality." And rightly so. But then, I have never even remotely claimed such.

To begin with, however, let us note that the Romantics who get so indignant about those two claims (some cultures being "inferior" and "lacking true spirituality") make exactly those claims themselves—not about foraging tribes, but about you and me. The general anthropological Romantic claim is that original tribal consciousness (during the period Gebser calls "magical") was "nondissociated," a type of harmony and wholeness of self, culture, and nature. The Romantic theorists agree that this magical structure was prereflexive and prerational (in the sense of pre-formal-operational thinking as a central organizing principle of society; the society was instead organized around prereflexive nondissociated consciousness). But, they claim, far from being a "lower" development, this prereflexive consciousness was balanced, holistic, ecologically sound, and deeply spiritual. But, they continue, with the eventual rise of egoic-rationality, this early nondissociated state was brutally repressed, fragmented, and destroyed; and in its place was a nightmare called modernity, which is marked, first and foremost, by *dissociated consciousness*, which carries alienation, fragmentation, and shallow (if any) spirituality. In other words, in its place are you and I: we moderns are all, with few exceptions, judged to be living in dissociated consciousness, an inferior, fragmented state, lacking a genuine spirituality.

This Romantic view thus condemns literally *hundreds of millions* of modern people as having inferior consciousness and lacking a deep spirituality. So the first thing we should note is that charges of "inferiority" and "lacking spirituality" drop from the lips of these Romantics with alarming ease and frequency. It is a very harsh system of ranking and value judgments that these Romantics have embraced, and it would do well for all of us to soften such brutal blows.

My view of the early tribal magical structure is, I believe, more nuanced. But let me first emphasize that I am talking about the original, prehistorical, tribal, foraging mode going back perhaps one or two million years ago. Indigenous peoples living today are people *living today*; they have continued to undergo their own development for hundreds of thousands of years, and their exact relationship to prehistoric tribes is far from clear; moreover, they are usually inextricably intermixed with other cultures and modes. No, I am referring to the structure of the original, prehistorical, magical-foraging mode, circa 50,000 B.C.E., to the extent we can reconstruct it.

To begin with, any society is a collection of individuals who themselves are at very different levels or stages of development. Just as today, where the average stage in industrial societies is something like egoic-rational, there are many individuals who are at higher and lower stages, and so also with earlier epochs. To say that a particular epoch was magical, or mythical, or mental, as Gebser does, is not to say that all individuals were at that level or stage. It's just an average.

This is why, as I pointed out in *Up from Eden,* any given culture has something like a "center of gravity," or an *average mode* of consciousness, around which conventional, everyday realities are organized (Foucault, for example, would call this "the dominant mode of discourse"). The Romantics agree that the average mode of early tribes was "magical" (in the nonpejorative sense of prereflexive and nondissociated) and the average mode of modernity is egoic-rational (which is usually meant pejoratively, but doesn't affect our main point about the average mode). I further suggested that in addition to the average mode, there is the *most advanced* mode, the mode displayed by those souls who appeared to be the most developed at that time (using any number of hermeneutically generated, non-meta-narrative vertical scales). During the magical-foraging times, the most advanced mode definitely appears to have included the shamans, who, I argued in *Up from Eden*, were the first great explorers of the genuinely transpersonal, spiritual domains. At the very least, these souls directly experienced the deeper psychic dimension of the human potential, evidenced in a sophisticated nature mysticism, journeys to upper- and underworld domains, what appear to be actual psychic capacities, and—again at the very least—a union consciousness with the entire realm of nature (or the gross/waking state). In *Up from Eden* I spent an entire chapter extolling these remarkable, authentic, and deeply spiritual feats.

At the same time, scholars of the shamanic state, such as Roger Walsh (*The Spirit of Shamanism*), have pointed out that, although there might have been exceptions, the typical shamanic voyage did not include, for example, extended periods of absorption in the purely formless realm (causal cessation). In other words, by criteria that are acceptable even to shamanic advocates, the shamanic voyage did not consciously include the causal domain. And therefore, at the very least, typical shamanic spirituality was not a path that traversed the entire transpersonal realm.

If, on the other hand, one performs (as *Up from Eden* did) a historical analysis on the succession or emergence of spiritual states accessed by the typical forms of the most advanced consciousness in each general epoch (magic to mythic to mental), one generally finds a succession of transpersonal states that move from shamanic (psychic) to saintly (subtle) to sagely (causal), with each of the succeeding states having access to their predecessors, but not vice versa—a true mark of a holarchy of development. States themselves do not generally show development, but increasing consciousness does, and that increase brought with it a more constant access of wakefulness to deeper and deeper domains, judging by the standards of those epochs themselves. (With the demise of transpersonal psychology, these criteria become even more pressing.)[11]

This leads to what I believe is the only model that so far has been able to adequately deal with evolution and enlightenment, and further, does so in a way that allows the most advanced mode of each epoch to be as enlightened as enlightened can be, and yet succeeding epochs could be more enlightened. It's a bit technical, so I will reserve it for an endnote, but I honestly can't think of a more important issue, certainly when it comes to spirituality and, hence, the human condition in general. If this topic interests you, I urge you to check the endnote and see if you agree or disagree with the suggested solution.¹²

To return to the *average mode* of the dawn state: What of the actual nature of the prereflexive, nondissociated consciousness, or the "magical structure" of the average mode of foraging consciousness? Was it truly an integrated, holistic, harmonious whole, as claimed by Romantics?

The magical structure, no doubt, was an extraordinary mode of consciousness; if nothing else, it inhabited the first men and women who evolved beyond the great apes and hominids, and although some people will insist on seeing this as an insult to apes, it was a colossal evolutionary advance by almost any scale of judgment. Still, the question is whether tribal consciousness actually *integrated* self, culture, and nature, or whether it had not yet fully differentiated them in the first place. By calling this magical structure "nondissociated," the Romantics beg the question, avoid the issue. The great, glorious, catchall prefix "non" always stands as a warning of a pre/post fallacy begging to be made. For the real question is not whether this structure was "nondifferentiated," but was this structure predifferentiated or was it truly postdifferentiated? "Nondissociated" can easily apply to both (which is how it hides its pre/post fallacy).

When we approach the question in this more careful fashion, the answer is more obvious: the magical structure was largely predifferentiated. On this, scholars from across a wide spectrum of approaches are in general agreement. Jean Houston, following Gerald Heard, calls this the pre-individual and proto-individual period (that is, archaic to magic). Duane Elgin refers to them as *constricted* consciousness and *proto*-consciousness. (This early state was one of *constricted* consciousness? Yes, and Elgin can spot this by not confusing the psychological fall with the metaphysical fall. Both early humans and early infants, who have suffered the metaphysical fall but not yet the psychological fall, are actually living in a very constricted, proto-state of consciousness, not a nondual state of union). Habermas and his colleagues, who conducted extensive research reviews, calls them preconventional and predifferentiated. Robert Bellah, tracing religious evolution, calls them primitive and archaic (predifferentiated action systems). Neumann called them pleromatic, uroboric, and pre-individuated. This does not mean stupid, confused, or imbecilic; it means that various subjective, objective, and intersubjective domains were not approached in fully differentiated terms. Some see this as a good thing; others as a problem; but there is general agreement on the actual nature of the structure itself.

The broad conclusion: with the magical structure, the self, culture, and nature still lay interfused with each other. They were not integrated, for they had not yet separated, differentiated, and crystallized out from each other. This predifferentiation is what gives the magical structure its, well, magical charm, and makes it a misunderstood magnet for those who actually desire a postdifferentiated integration for the modern world. But the actual situation of the foraging mode was, apart from its occasional wonders, something less than an integrated paradise. Because the "I," the "we," and the "it" were as yet poorly differentiated, advances in each domain were hindered. Average life span was less than three decades; political systems were focused on body-bound kinship lineages; slavery was sporadic but already occurring (showing that it is intrinsic in the nondissociated mode); warfare had already begun; and sexual exploitation was often rampant. It is, *in its complete contours*, a consciousness that no Romantic I know would actually want to inhabit.

A Clearer Picture Has Recently Emerged

Although the somewhat dismal picture I have painted of the average magical, foraging, nondissociated consciousness could be discerned at least two decades ago, to do so would have subverted what had already become the dominant mode of academic discourse, and hence books like *Up from Eden* and *A Sociable God* were aggressively attacked. Today, as the boomeritis hangover is slowly wearing off, this more accurate picture is now becoming more commonly acknowledged.

A good example is Michael Crichton, Harvard-graduated M.D. known for the careful scholarship he brings to books such as *Jurassic Park* and *Timeline*. Crichton gives a superb summary of the evidence as it now exists, delivered through his own slightly exasperated tone at how long this evidence has been distorted due to what he calls a religious denial of facts (the "religion" in this case being the religious dogma of ecoprimitivism, using definition number 8 of the word "religion" as outlined in *A Sociable God*). Here are excerpts from Crichton's summary; although Crichton is not a scholar of these issues, he does a superb job of summarizing the scholarly consensus that has emerged in this area:

> There is no Eden. There never was. What was that Eden of the wonderful mythic past? Is it the time when infant mortality was

80%, when four children in five died of disease before the age of five? When one woman in six died in childbirth? When the average lifespan was 40, as it was in America a century ago? When plagues swept across the planet, killing millions in a stroke. Was it when millions starved to death? Is that when it was Eden?

And what about indigenous peoples, living in a state of harmony with the Eden-like environment? Well, they never did. On this continent, the newly arrived people who crossed the land bridge almost immediately set about wiping out hundreds of species of large animals, and they did this several thousand years before the white man showed up, to accelerate the process. And what was the condition of life? Loving, peaceful, harmonious? Hardly: the early peoples of the New World lived in a state of constant warfare. Generations of hatred, tribal hatreds, constant battles. The warlike tribes of this continent are famous: the Comanche, Sioux, Apache, Mohawk, Aztecs, Toltec, Incas. Some of them practiced infanticide, and human sacrifice. And those tribes that were not fiercely warlike were exterminated, or learned to build their villages high in the cliffs to attain some measure of safety.

How about the human condition in the rest of the world? The Maori of New Zealand committed massacres regularly. The Dyaks of Borneo were headhunters. The Polynesians, living in an environment as close to paradise as one can imagine, fought constantly, and created a society so hideously restrictive that you could lose your life if you stepped in the footprint of a chief. It was the Polynesians who gave us the very concept of taboo, as well as the word itself. The noble savage is a fantasy, and it was never true. That anyone still believes it, 200 years after Rousseau, shows the tenacity of religious myths, their ability to hang on in the face of centuries of factual contradiction.

There was even an academic movement, during the latter 20th century, that claimed that cannibalism was a white man's invention to demonize the indigenous peoples. (Only academics could fight such a battle.) It was some thirty years before professors finally agreed that yes, cannibalism does indeed occur among human beings. Meanwhile, all during this time New Guinea highlanders in the 20th century continued to eat the brains of their enemies until they were finally made to understand that they risked kuru, a fatal neurological disease, when they did so.

More recently still the gentle Tasaday of the Philippines turned out to be a publicity stunt, a nonexistent tribe. And African pygmies have one of the highest murder rates on the planet.

In short, the romantic view of the natural world as a blissful Eden is only held by people who have no actual experience of nature. People who live in nature are not romantic about it at all. They may hold spiritual beliefs about the world around them, they may have a sense of the unity of nature or the aliveness of all things, but they still kill the animals and uproot the plants in order to eat, to live. If they don't, they will die.

Crichton goes on to comment pointedly on the Romantic disposition behind the myths:

And if you, even now, put yourself in nature even for a matter of days, you will quickly be disabused of all your romantic fantasies. Take a trek through the jungles of Borneo, and in short order you will have festering sores on your skin, you'll have bugs all over your body, biting in your hair, crawling up your nose and into your ears, you'll have infections and sickness and if you're not with somebody who knows what they're doing, you'll quickly starve to death. But chances are that even in the jungles of Borneo you won't experience nature so directly, because you will have covered your entire body with DEET and you will be doing everything you can to keep those bugs off you.

The truth is, almost nobody wants to experience real nature. What people want is to spend a week or two in a cabin in the woods, with screens on the windows. They want a simplified life for a while, without all their stuff. Or a nice river rafting trip for a few days, with somebody else doing the cooking. Nobody wants to go back to nature in any real way, and nobody does. It's all talk—and as the years go on, and the world population grows increasingly urban, it's uninformed talk. Farmers know what they're talking about. City people don't. It's all fantasy.

Eden is a fantasy that never existed, and mankind wasn't ever noble and kind and loving, [and] we didn't fall from grace [because we were never historically in paradise to begin with]. . . .

In that regard, I wonder if anybody has ever pointed out that the early foraging tribes, supposedly living in paradisical nondissociated consciousness, were themselves the ones who abandoned that state and moved into horticultural and agrarian (and "fallen") modes. If the original state was so paradisical, why did the tribes themselves abandon paradise? How smart could they actually have been if that were so? If the Romantics are right and the early tribes were living in a total paradise that they intentionally abandoned, then those tribes were without doubt the stupidest human beings who ever lived. But of course they weren't stupid—far from it, they abandoned paradise for a reason, which is that "paradise" it most certainly was not.

The Basic Inadequacy of Foraging Consciousness

The fact that magic could be taken up and into mythic, and mythic could be taken up and into mental, is a development that—ideally—would carry the extraordinary accomplishments of each mode forward, building on their strengths, curtailing their partialness, and building together a more embracing, inclusive, encompassing future. Ideally, evolution occurs through a process of "transcend and include"—transcend the previous stage's limitations but include its accomplishments.

But no development or evolution is without its possible pathologies. Cultural evolution is no exception; it has as often been the history of brutalities, repressions, oppressions, and worse, as human evolution sometimes progressed, sometimes brutalized, its way toward tomorrow. *Up from Eden* was a chronicle of the undeniable advances, and the even more undeniable brutalities.

But the general point of phylogenetic evolution, as of ontogenetic, is that *whenever the wisdom of a previous stage is forgotten, a pathology results*. In *A Brief History of Everything* I outlined the major "lessons" that each age of humanity managed to learn, and the point here is that the great foraging lesson was: *Spirit is interwoven with earthbody*, which is our blood, our bones, our foundation, our support. We of the modern West have forgotten that lesson, and we are therefore in the grips of a global pathology that very well might kill us all.

But what the magical, preconventional structure could not do—and still cannot do—is integrate other magical structures. That is, magic is cognitively not complex enough to build intersubjective structures that would allow mutual understanding among hundreds of different tribes. And therefore, the magical structure, even if it did know how to honor gross-realm nature (a claim itself disputed),[13] could not build the types of consensus necessary for human beings to live in harmony with nature. Thus, the magical structure, even if it honored nature, could never protect nature. This protection would require centauric, not typhonic, awareness—that is, postconventional intersubjective consensus across thousands, even millions, of kinship lines, and not merely subjective, preconventional, tribal feelings in the present moment.

Likewise, it is quite beyond the capacity of the magical-foraging structure to actually honor Gaia, since Gaia is a systemic conception. As Clare Graves pointed out, with the magical-animistic structure, "there is a name for every bend in the river, but no name for the river." And thus Gaia is likewise a nonentity for tribal awareness. There is a name for every nook and cranny in Gaia, but no Gaia itself. Magical nondissociated consciousness is indeed constricted consciousness; it is the particularistic, immediate, present, and naive moment in front of its face. Hence Habermas is certainly correct to conclude that the foraging structure is essentially egocentric and preconventional in its nature.

That the Romantics want us to remember the positive contributions of that early structure is very much to their credit, and in that specific regard, I am a staunch Romantic. But when they go quite beyond that and dubiously inject characteristics into the magical nondissociated structure—when they claim postdifferentiated integration for what most scholars would see as predifferentiated structures; when they claim the shamanic voyage was a complete path across the transpersonal; when they claim that the mental-rational structure itself is intrinsically pathological; when they confuse immediate vital impulses for Gaia systemic networks; and when they toxically condemn millions of people to living in an inferior state compared with magical indissociation—perhaps we might not wish to follow them.[14]

FALLING, FALLING, FALLING . . . FALLEN

We have been using Carol Gilligan's scale (egocentric/selfish, ethnocentric/care, worldcentric/universal care, integrated) as a simple example of a vertical dimension of developmental depth (constructed as a conscious hermeneutic and not as an exterior meta-narrative). *A Sociable God* uses a slightly more sophisticated (but still relatively simple) outline of the general spectrum of consciousness, focusing primarily on worldviews (archaic, magic, mythic, mental, psychic, subtle, causal, nondual). In addition to giving at least a dozen or so different ways that the word "religion" is commonly used, it then points out that, at the very least, we need to distinguish between horizontal *legitimacy* (or how well a given spirituality provides meaning, integration, and value at a particular level) and vertical *authenticity* (or how well a given spirituality promotes transformation to higher levels altogether).[15] Most religious scholars, in confusing these two scales, have seen the loss or disruption of a lower-level engagement that happened to be highly legitimate, and mistaken that for a loss of spiritual sensibilities altogether, when in fact it was merely part of a larger movement to a more authentic stance.

We just saw that those scholars who are fond of the magical, foraging, nondissociated fusion state tend to see every succeeding stage—starting with mythic—as a catastrophic fall from an original paradise. Likewise, scholars who believe that the mythic structure was actually the original paradise tend to see the rise of the next major structure, the rational-egoic, as the eating of the tree of knowledge and the real fall of man. And it doesn't stop there. Those who see the modern world of science as the closest thing we have to paradise tend to see the rise of the next major structure—which might be called the planetsoul—as being a throwback to magical superstition (i.e., their version of the Fall).

What's going on here? In various books, starting with *Up from Eden* and *A Sociable God*, I have tried to suggest three major items that have contributed to this incredibly widespread tendency to see every stage past your favorite as the Fall of humankind. These factors are: (1) a confusion of the metaphysical fall and the psychological fall;[16] (2) a confusion of differentiation and dissociation; (3) a tendency to see Spirit as being present in one epoch and not in others, instead of seeing Spirit present as the entire evolutionary unfolding.

A confusion of differentiation and dissociation can be particularly pernicious. Growth and development generally occur through a process of differentiation-and-integration. But if you believe that the early dawn state is a state of spiritual oneness (albeit unconscious), then you will see every differentiation as a fragmentation, a breaking, an alienation. You will thoroughly confuse necessary differentiation with pathological dissociation, with a fall of some sort. And thus, if your favorite period is magical-foraging, you will see the mythic-agrarian as the great Fall of humankind, the beginning of the rape of nature via planting and harvesting. If you see mythical Eden as paradise, you will see the rise of modernity as the great Fall. If you are a rational scientist, you will see a coming postformal, postrational state as a horrifying Fall, and so on. Differentiation-and-integration—which is part of the means of growth and evolution to higher, wider, deeper, more unified states—appears to be a continuous fragmentation and moving away from the simple fusion state, which indeed it is, but that cannot be appreciated if that simple fusion state has been identified with nirvana. Once that confusion occurs, the means of growth appears to be part of the illness. You then view every new stage of deeper evolution with horror and disgust: the Fall! the Fall! the Fall of humankind!

Having confused differentiation and dissociation, we will once again imagine that the earlier stages of evolution represent a spiritual oneness that is subsequently lost, that Spirit was available at one stage or epoch and not at others, instead of seeing that Spirit is the entire sweep of the evolutionary unfolding. Spirit is the Ground of the entire evolutionary sequence; it does not pop into existence at one epoch, say hello, then disappear at another.

Those three confusions contribute, I believe, to so many intense misunderstandings about Spirit and history, that only an integral approach can even begin to unravel them. *A Sociable God* is a step in that direction, and this is one of its substantial merits, I believe.

THE RATIONALIZATION OF SECULAR SOCIETY

Where religious scholars are busy seeing a series of falls of humankind as it rushes into the modern world, secular scholars are busy seeing a progressive enlightenment and overcoming of superstition with the rise of modernity, science, and liberalization. Who is right?

In a sense, both of them, of course. Or, as we say, both of them are half right, half wrong. Religious scholars are correct in that almost every stage of development past their favorite era is a fall, at least from that favorite era. If, for example, you equate religion with mythic legitimacy (or dogmatic mythic beliefs, as in the Virgin Birth and the parting of the Red Sea), then the rise of modernity must indeed appear to be antispiritual. If, on the other hand, you see evolution as Spirit-in-action, then the rise of modernity in its healthy form is simply an increase in differentiation-and-integration, an increase in Spirit's presence. Spirit has simply moved from magic to mythic to rational, on its way to even further, postrational unfoldments. The irony here is that the rise of modernity is actually an increase in spiritual unfolding, but Spirit resides now not in myths but in reason. There is more Spirit in reason's denial of a mythic God than there is in myth's affirmation of that God.

On the other hand, what both myth and reason have misunderstood is that, wherever one might wish to locate Spirit, everybody is born at square one. The great secularization of society, predicted by rational scholars for two centuries, has simply not occurred—not, anyway, in a fashion resembling anything that was predicted. It was thought that modern society would become less and less religious (and here, "religious" specifically means magic and mythic). The idea was that scientific, enlightened, rational progress would *entirely* erase magic and mythic silliness, leaving a rational-secular society top to bottom.

In some ways, there has indeed been an increase in the percentage of the population that is rational-secular; many governing institutions embrace a separation of church and state (where church usually means magic and mythic and state means rational); educational systems likewise are often liberal-rational (the more educated a person becomes, the less magic and mythic they embrace). Thus, large stretches of industrial developed countries are indeed rational-secular, and long gone are the times that an explicit Holy (Mythic) Roman Empire could count on a consensus.

But magic and mythic have not simply evaporated. The reason they have not is that everybody is born at archaic, then hits magic, then mythic, then rational. And hence, for every person who moves into rational, there is often one or more who enter mythic. Accordingly, even in rational-secular societies, large pockets of culture remain at prerational stages of unfolding (and always will to some degree, because everybody is born at square one). People are free to stop growing whenever they want, as long as they do not harm others. There will always be pockets of culture in this society that are archaic, magic, and mythic.

Not to mention the vast majority of second- and third-world cultures, at this time anyway, where magic and mythic often dominate. Further, given that magical-tribal and mythic-ethnocentric stages of development appear in their true colors as terrorists, warlords, feudalistic empires, ethnic cleansing, among others, those difficulties will continue to plague the planet. Even if the center of gravity of the world's population were rational or higher, pockets of prerational culture would continue to exist and must be handled with specific legal, political, and occasionally military means. (See "The Deconstruction of the World Trade Center," at http://wilber.shambhala.com, for further discussion of this pressing issue.)

A Sociable God points out that, even if we focus on the average mode of industrial-informational societies—that of egoic-rational—then the further evolution of that mode will bring surprises to even those who see modernity as an antispiritual movement; namely, beyond the rational are the postrational stages of development (which are *not* antirational but indeed postrational, or transcending-and-including rationality). Hence, even the rise of rationality is a movement of Spirit-in-action leading to even more obviously spiritual modes. If, of course, we survive to tell the tale. . . .

Thus, *A Sociable God* suggests that the loss of the hegemony of a mythic-membership religion with the rise of modernity, a loss so audibly lamented by mythic religion, was not actually the loss of a transrational spirituality and its replacement by the devil of rationality, but was mostly the growth beyond prerational modes to rational modes *on the way to* the transrational. As we were saying, in this larger evolutionary view, the rational denial of God contained more Spirit than the mythic affirmation of God, for the simple reason that it contained more developmental depth (and thus, in fact, more Spirit). It was more authentic, even if it was occasionally less legitimate—it was a sick version of a higher level, compared to the previous healthy version of a lower level, so as we attempt to redress the ills of modernity, let us not forget the higher potential contained therein.

DEPTH AND DIVINITY

The criteria for depth—and the *scale of adjudication* used in *A Sociable God* (as in all of my works)—is *holistic embrace*: how much of the Kosmos can a given structure internally contain? Put objectively, how many types of holons does a particular self-organizing system contain in its own makeup? Put subjectively, how much love (Agape) is built into a structure?

A holon is a whole that is a part of other wholes. A quark is enfolded in an atom; an atom is enfolded in a molecule; a molecule into a cell; a cell into an organism. In each case, the holon gains more *depth*, because it lovingly embraces more of the Kosmos in its own makeup. Likewise with human holons: when my identity and sympathy expand from me to my family; from my family to tribes, communities, even nations; from nations to all of humanity; and from humanity to all sentient beings without exception: what have I done?, except take more and more souls into my own, and increased thereby my own depth, by moving increasingly out of me and into the Kosmos at large, until what I call my "self" and what I call the "Kosmos" are one and the same undeniable Fact, and the Love that moves the sun and other stars now moves me just as well; and we are all embraced in a gentle compassion that knows no others or outsiders, that refuses fragmentation and cannot remember sorrow's many names.

That scale—from egocentric to ethnocentric to worldcentric to Kosmic—is a scale of holistic embrace, and that scale is the one used in *A Sociable God* to adjudicate the authenticity of various cultural and religious engagements. Each higher embrace does not mean that individuality is increasingly obliterated, but that it is increasingly enlarged. A person who extends sympathy and caring from his own ego to his family, and from his family to his community, has not impoverished his self, but enriched it. Just so, to expand one's identity and sympathy from tribe to multi-tribe nation, and from nation to all humanity, and from humanity to all sentient beings—is simply to find a deeper Self in the midst of wider embraces. Kosmic consciousness is not the obliteration of individuality, but its consummate fulfillment, at which point we can speak of big Self or no-self, it matters not which: your Self is the Self of the entire Kosmos, timeless and therefore eternal, spaceless and therefore infinite, moved only by a radiant Love that defies date or duration.

That holarchy, or nest of increasingly holistic judgments, has been central to every work I have ever written, starting with my first book, *The Spectrum of Consciousness*; and of course it was as well the backbone of *A Sociable God*, which was written right at the beginning of the eighties—right at the beginning, we have been pointing out, of the colonization of cultural studies by flatland postmodernists. As we have also been pointing out, it would be almost two decades before anybody could breathe the word "hierarchy" and not be lynched in academia; before anybody could murmur the phrase "is better than" and not be brought before the postmodern tribunal and publicly branded a heretic. For the core of extreme postmodernism was the notion that all values are culturally relative; all realities are socially constructed; all truth is a subjective preference or taste. Unfortunately, all of those statements are said to be true *for all people and for all cultures*, without exception. In other words, the extreme postmodernists were guilty of exactly the horrible sins they accused everybody else of: they pronounced a long list of *universal truths*, but with the further embarrassment that their universal truths were all self-contradictory. They claimed it was universally true that there are no universal truths, that it is a cultural invariant that there are no cultural invariants, that it is objectively true that there is no objective truth. They claimed, in short, that their position was superior in a world where nothing was supposed to be superior. Critics would eventually spot this duplicity and give it a technical moniker—"the performative contradiction"—but others would simply call it by its simpler name, hypocrisy.

And now, as cultural studies itself begins to shake off its dogmatism—an entire generation of scholarship largely lost in performative contradictions, in narcissism and nihilism as a postmodern tag team from hell—we are in a position to pick up exactly where holistic and nested hierarchies and value judgments left off: with ways of determining how to make sane, compassionate, and caring judgments based on degrees of depth, on degrees of love, on degrees of inclusion and holistic embrace. Pick up, that is, where numerous treatises, including *A Sociable God*, left off.

THE INTEGRAL APPROACH

A Sociable God and *Up from Eden* are books that particularly explored cultural worldviews. I would later come to call this the Lower-Left quadrant (the spectrum of collective or cultural consciousness, morals, worldviews, etc.). *The Atman Project* had already attempted to outline the Upper-Left quadrant (or the individual spectrum of consciousness). What both *Up from Eden* and *A Sociable God* further accomplished, I believe, was to *tie these two quadrants together*, and to believably show that the individual and the cultural *are inextricably bound by patterns of relational exchange*. That is, the human being is a compound individual, compounded of matter, body, mind, soul, and spirit (to use a simple five-level scheme). Each level of the compound individual is actually *a system of mutual exchange* with elements *at the same level of development* (i.e., *the same degree of depth*) in the exterior world: matter with matter (physical food consumption), body with body (sexual procreation), mind with mind (symbolic communication), and so on. At every level, in other words, the subjective world is embedded in vast networks of intersubjective or cultural relationships, and vice versa, not as an afterthought or a voluntary choice, but as an inescapable pregiven fact. As I would later put it, agency is always agency-in-communion.

It is common to look at social evolution in terms of the various modes of techno-economic production, moving from foraging to horticultural to agrarian to industrial to informational (what I would call the Lower-Right quadrant, or social systems). By supplementing that analysis with a focus on *worldviews* (which move correlatively from archaic to magic to mythic to mental to global),[17] *A Sociable God* was able to make a series of predictions that have held up quite well. One was that the breakdown of the civil religion (as discussed by Robert Bellah) would leave American culture open to several trends, including a retrenchment and even resurgence of fundamentalist religion, as well as a regression to narcissistic New Age agendas and intense self-absorption (a resurgence of Romanticism in its unhealthy forms). It's not hard to find corroborative evidence for both of those in today's culture. But another, riskier prediction involved the fact that beyond the rational-egoic (and centauric) level is the first stage of postrationality, referred to in *A Sociable God* (somewhat unhappily) as the psychic level, which supports a panenhenic nature mysticism. The prediction was that the most widespread, popular themes of a newly emerging spiritual orientation would therefore involve panenhenic nature mysticism and Gaia worship, along with a considerably reinterpreted shamanism, focused on ecological consciousness and gross realm unity. More than I imagined, this has become the case.

On the one hand, this is altogether salutary, coming just in time, one hopes, to help stem a certain ecological catastrophe wrought, not by modernity per se, but by typical human greed, a greed that—most definitely present from the time of archaic foraging, but which at that time had not the means to express itself globally—finally found a way, by hijacking the fruits of modernity, to make itself suicidal on a global scale.

Alas, with this resurgence of nature mysticism has also come the standard, correlative distrust of all higher mystical states, including deity mysticism and formless mysticism. These are, as always, misinterpreted by panenhenic enthusiasts to be "other-worldly" and therefore supposedly anti-earth, anti-Gaia, and anti-ecological, whereas they actually transcend and include all of those concerns. But the nature mystics have often come armed with venomous words for souls who seek yet deeper and higher occasions, and I believe it will be decades before this particular fury runs its unpleasant course.[18]

It was by focusing on a developmental and evolutionary view of consciousness that these books (especially *Up from Eden* and *A Sociable*

God) were able, I believe, to contribute to an understanding of these various movements. Toward the end of this period I began, not so much to question the evolutionary model, as to appreciate both its strengths and its weaknesses. In particular, studies in developmental psychology were already starting to suggest that development does not proceed in a linear fashion through a series of discrete ladder-like stages. Rather, overall development seems to consist of numerous different developmental lines or streams (such as cognitive, moral, affective, psychological, and spiritual) that progress in a relatively independent fashion through the basic spectrum of consciousness. If we simplify the spectrum of consciousness as going from preconventional to conventional to post-conventional to post-postconventional waves, and if we use affects or feelings as an example of a particular stream, then we have *preconventional affects* (e.g., narcissistic rage, impulse gratification), *conventional affects* (belongingness, care, concern), *postconventional affects* (universal love, global altruism), and *post-postconventional affects* (transpersonal compassion, love-bliss, Kosmic care). Likewise with cognition, morals, needs, psychological (or self) development, and spiritual development (considered as a separate line), among many others.

Each of these developmental lines or streams traverses the same basic levels or waves, but each does so in a relatively independent fashion, so that, for example, a person can be at a very high level of cognitive development, a medium level of interpersonal development, and a low level of moral development, all at the same time. This shows how truly uneven and non-linear overall development can be. A massive amount of research continued to demonstrate that the individual developmental lines themselves unfold in a sequential manner—the important truth discovered by developmental studies. But since there are at least a dozen different developmental lines, overall growth itself shows no such sequential development, but is instead a radically uneven and individual affair. Moreover, at any given time a particular individual might show much growth in one stream (say, psychological), while showing little or no growth in others (say, spiritual). None of this could be explained by a single-stream evolutionary model, but all of it made perfect sense according to a levels-and-lines model (so-called phase-3).

Although I abandoned the strictly linear or "ladder-like" view of development by 1981, I am criticized to this day for presenting a rigidly linear view of development, where, it is alleged, psychological development must be fully complete before spiritual development can even begin. I never held that rigid a view even in phase-1, and I certainly abandoned anything remotely like that almost two decades ago.[19] So I never know quite how to respond to these charges, other than to point out that they are untrue.

With the publication of *Sex, Ecology, Spirituality* in 1995, I believe that the integral approach came to a full fruition. The follow-up books to SES included *A Brief History of Everything, The Marriage of Sense and Soul, Integral Psychology, One Taste, A Theory of Everything,* and *Boomeritis.* Those books present an integral model that includes quadrants, levels, lines, states, and types, and that, taken together, cover some of the most important cross-cultural elements that any approach aspiring to be comprehensive or integral ought to take into account. If you would like to see how the worldviews investigated by *Up from Eden* and *A Sociable God* are an important part of the integral model, I would suggest you start by reading the short introduction *A Theory of Everything.*

In the meantime, here are a few quadrant diagrams summarizing the essential points. "Quadrants" are simply four perspectives that are especially important in viewing any occasion: *any event can be looked at from the inside and from the outside, and in the singular and the plural.* That simple statement, were it accepted, would put an end to ninety percent of academic food fights. Zero chance that will happen, but it's still nice to know that methodological peace might actually be available for those so inclined.

In any event, these four basic perspectives show us quite different phenomena, all of which are part of the integral picture. On the accompanying diagrams, the *interior of the individual* is represented in the *Upper-Left quadrant* (UL), including the perspectives of first person singular ("I"). The *interior of the plural (or the collective)* is the *Lower-Left quadrant* (LL), including second person ("you/thou") and first-person plural ("we"). The *exterior of the individual* is the *Upper-Right quadrant* (UR), including third-person singular ("it"). And the *exterior of the collective* is the *Lower-Right quadrant* (LR), including third-person plural ("its"). We sometimes shorten these to three major domains: I, we, and it; or the Beautiful, the Good, and the True; or art, morals, and science.

Diagram 1 is a typical quadrant figure representing some of the more common elements (or holons) that are disclosed by these four perspectives to a human being at a vision-logic (integrated or higher) level of development. It is fairly self-explanatory. The UL quadrant shows thirteen major waves of development instead of the four simple ones we

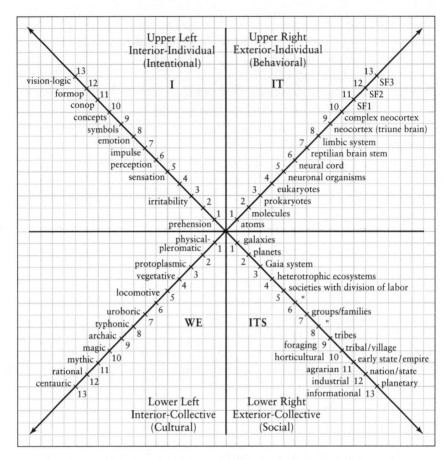

DIAGRAM 1. Typical quadrants.

have been using; and the LL shows a similar enhancement of the world-views of archaic, magic, mythic, rational, integral (centauric and higher), but all of them should be recognizable as variations on a theme.

Diagram 2 is a quadrant diagram focusing specifically on human beings, using the research of Clare Graves as a simple example of some of the levels or stages of development in the UL. We have been using Carol Gilligan's four stages of selfish (beige, purple, red), care (blue), universal care (orange, green), and integrated (yellow, turquoise), which are generally correlated with the more specific Graves stages as indicated in parentheses. If you are interested in these types of stage correlations and the substantial amount of research that developmentalists have done over the years, please consult *Integral Psychology*, which gives tables

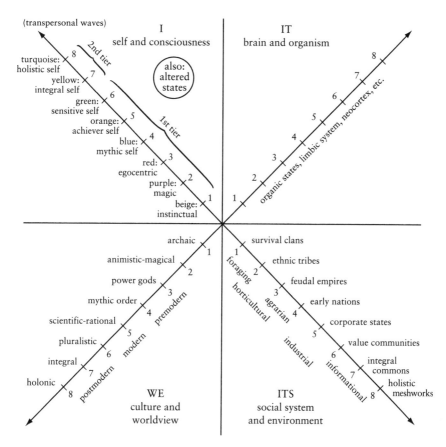

DIAGRAM 2. Quadrants focusing specifically on human beings.

showing over one hundred developmental models and their general correlations.

Notice in diagram 2 that the UL contains the words "also: altered states." The point here is that we can indeed map those altered *states* of consciousness (gross, subtle, causal, nondual) against the *stages* of consciousness represented in this diagram by the Graves stages, to result in a Wilber-Combs matrix of possible religious/spiritual experiences. This is the type of interpretive analytic pioneered by *A Sociable God*.

Notice also that, when it comes to the orthodox versions of today's sociology of religion, there are two major camps: the hermeneuticists and the functionalists. *A Sociable God* gives several reasons why both of them must be included in any integral picture, and using a quadrant diagram we can easily see why: those two major approaches often focus, respectively, on the *Lower-Left quadrant* and the *Lower-Right quadrant*. It goes without saying that both are crucial components of any integral approach.

Eight Primordial Perspectives of Sentient Beings

Allow me to conclude this preface by schematically summarizing *integral methodological pluralism*, as in diagrams 3 and 4.

Diagram 3 simply names the inside and outside of an event in each of the four quadrants. That is, we can take any of the occasions that are disclosed by the perspectives of the quadrants, and we can add yet another perspective, namely: are we attempting to look at it from its own

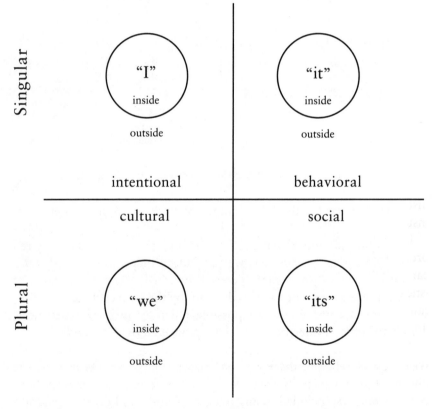

DIAGRAM 3. Eight primordial perspectives of sentient beings.

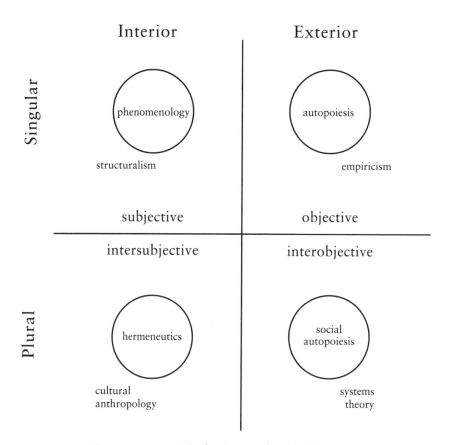

DIAGRAM 4. Eight fundamental methodologies.

inside or from its own outside? This gives us eight major perspectives instead of the simpler four.

I believe these *eight major perspectives* are the fewest that we need in order to get a fairly well-rounded view of any occasion. Of course we can use more; and we certainly can use fewer (and not merely reductionistically, but perhaps for introductory purposes, where the four quadrants serve wonderfully). But use fewer than eight and some very important variables get left out.

My work in the last few years has been to develop a Kosmology that replaces things, events, perceivers, systems, and processes with two simple variables: sentient beings and their perspectives. Assuming that the universe contains sentient beings and their perspectives, we can easily generate things, systems, processes, perceivers, knowers, thinkers, events, dynamic processes, and so on, simply by specifying which perspective is being inhabited when the entity in question is being asserted. The entire metaphysical approach to reality—including not only the overt and obvious metaphysics of the great wisdom traditions but the *hidden metaphysics* of everything from systems theory to postmodernism—is supplanted by a radically post-metaphysical approach that no longer assumes the fundamentalness of systems or processes or events or perceivers or knowers or dharmas or anything—except sentient beings and their perspectives on other sentient beings.

These primordial perspectives (which spring into being whenever there is a plural of any sort of sentience or prehension) turn out to be the underpinnings of the Integral Methodological Pluralism that drove me into dishwashing. If you look at diagram 4, you can see that these eight primordial perspectives drive eight of the most widely used, most time-tested of all human methodologies, from empiricism to phenomenology to hermeneutics to systems theory to developmentalism.

For example, if we look at the interior of an "I" from its own inside, we get introspection, phenomenology, meditation, and so on—we are looking at an "I" from within. But we can study that "I" from without as well (or in an "objective" or third-person fashion), and one of the results of doing that would be seeing the various stages of development that this "I" might go through (which is exactly what Carol Gilligan and Clare Graves did, for example, using the techniques of structuralism—in this case, developmental structuralism).

Likewise, we can look at any "we" from its own inside—hermeneutics, participant observer, sympathetic resonance—or we can study it from without, in an anthropological disposition (which is still nevertheless focused on meaning, genealogy, and semantics; still, that is, focused on the LL quadrant). But we can also look at that cultural "we" from an "objective" or third-person perspective, as a social system of dynamically interwoven "its"—the LR quadrant of systems theory (systems that themselves can be viewed from their own within as autopoietic or self-making systems, or more traditionally from their own without as structural-functional systems). The simple point is that the (at least) eight major perspectives available to sentient beings underpin the (at least) eight major methodologies that any truly integral approach would want to include.

And the wholesale disaster, the jarring nightmare, is that, academically, these are the eight major perspectives and methodologies, one or more of which are always getting outlawed, marginalized, repressed, oppressed, and tossed in the garbage can of no-no, nasty, don't-touch-this injunctions.

Which is what drove me into dishwashing as a preferable job. Looking back on the thirty years of my life as a methodological outlaw—where "outlaw," by the way, is defined exactly as it is in *A Sociable God*—it seems that with virtually every one of the two dozen scholarly books I have written, academia has often recoiled in horror, and has done so, when it has done so, for the same basic reason, which has never varied very much: I was befriending some methodology or another that was deemed unrespectable. Their motto was never, "Everybody is right," because both the culture and more sadly the counterculture had their narrow lists of right thinkers and their longer lists of thought criminals (to use George Orwell's wonderful wording). Dishwashing wasn't so bad, compared to all of that.

Diagram 4 is a summary of the methodologies I was befriending and using all the way back to my first book; it just took me thirty years to explicate what was involved. That first book, by the way, written at age twenty-three and called *The Spectrum of Consciousness*, might as well have been titled *The Spectrum of Methodologies*, *The Spectrum of Paradigms*, *The Spectrum of Injunctions*, since that is what was actually involved. But most authorities in the culture and counterculture, I found, do not want to look through new telescopes because they already know that Jupiter has no moons.

Like I said, dishwashing. I was, incidentally, still washing dishes at the Red Rooster Restaurant when I wrote *A Sociable God*. Its major point was simply that *a sociology of depth* would have to include *vertical interiors*, both individual and collective—in other words, would have to include the results of such methodologies as developmental structuralism and phenomenology in addition to systems theory and hermeneutics (see diagram 4). I stand behind that conclusion one hundred percent. For the succinct and elegant way that it argues for such a vertical dimension, *A Sociable God* remains a clarion call for a greater sociology.

INTEGRAL TODAY

The success of the integral model has itself been inspiring: www.integralnaked.org, www.integraluniversity.com, and www.integralinstitute.org are all flourishing. If you would like to be involved in the application of a more inclusive, comprehensive, integral approach to any human endeavor—including integral medicine, integral art, integral law, integral psychotherapy, integral business, integral politics, integral education—please start at www.integralinstitute.org and join us in this exciting adventure of expanding care and consciousness.

KEN WILBER
Denver, Colorado
Summer 2004

NOTES

1. For the reasons that developmental holism (or structural developmentalism) is not a meta-narrative imposed on a group from without, but is rather a genealogical hermeneutic generated from within the consensus circle of those being questioned, see http://wilber.shambhala.com, Sidebar A, "Who Ate Captain Cook? Historiography in a Postmodern World."

Developmental holism is a variety of "zone-2" methodology, or the third-person study of first-person plural realities (see http://wilber.shambhala.com, Excerpts A through G, from *Sex, Karma, and Creativity*, the follow-up volume to *Sex, Ecology, Spirituality*).

2. The reasons for the distortions of Thomas Kuhn's work, particularly *The Structure of Scientific Revolutions*, as well as Gilligan's, are explored at length in *Boomeritis*.

3. For a fully developed notion of three-dimensional feminism, please see chapter 8, "Integral Feminism," in *The Eye of Spirit*, which is, to my knowledge, the first essay ever written on integral feminism.

4. See *The Eye of Spirit* and *Integral Psychology*.

5. Hazrat Inayat Khan represents the former version, that of reincarnation, as follows: "The crying of an infant is very often the expression of its longing for the angelic heavens [through which it has just passed on its way to earthly birth—what the Tibetans call the rebirth bardo]; the smiles of an infant are a narrative of its memories of heaven and of the spheres above." That is what I call "the trailing clouds of glory," from a Wordsworth poem (see *The Eye of Spirit* for an extensive discussion of this idea). But notice that these potentials are not something that are part of the infantile stage or structure itself—they are lingering impressions from other, *higher* spheres. And therefore, what is *recaptured* in enlightenment is *not* the infantile structure itself, but the actual higher spheres! The Romantic notion that the infantile self *is itself* a primordial paradise remains therefore deeply mistaken.

See the Introduction to volume 3 of the *Collected Works* and *The Eye of Spirit* for further discussion.

6. Caution: *A Sociable God* still tends to speak of a type of peak experience or glimpse experience of higher structures/stages, although it is careful to always speak of higher realms or higher dimensions, thus never being technically incorrect (i.e.,

"higher realms" and "higher dimensions" can and often do refer to higher states and their bodies, the major ones of which—such as waking/gross, dreaming/subtle, and sleep/causal—are ever-present in many respects and therefore can be peak experienced). But let us be clear: although some higher states can be peak experienced, higher stages cannot.

Still, what *A Sociable God* does is present the first form of what is now called the Wilber-Combs matrix, where dimensions/states/realms that are being experienced are mapped against the stages/structures that are interpreting the experiences. This is a genuinely novel and important breakthrough, I believe.

7. The infant certainly has access to what I refer to as the three major states of consciousness: gross (waking), subtle (dreaming and deeper psychic), and causal (deep sleep, pure Witness, primordial Self). The early self (prenatal, perinatal, neonatal, infancy, and early childhood) has various types of access to all of those spiritual states. But so does the adult. In other words, the infantile state, in this regard, does not have access to something spiritual that is then *necessarily lost* or denied to the adult. (The strictly Romantic view is, again, significantly off the mark.)

So does the infantile self have access to any sort of "spiritual awareness" that is actually *lost* in subsequent development but can be *regained* in higher states of spiritual awakening? In a limited sense, yes: the trailing clouds of glory (whether in their prenatal, perinatal, neonatal, or later forms). But, to repeat, those traditions that acknowledge the "trailing clouds" insist that those are primarily a lingering contact or impression of higher, transpersonal, transrational levels; they are *not* potentials that are structurally part of the infantile self, so that in recontacting these higher levels in subsequent development, it is not a *regression* to infancy that is occurring, but a *progression* to, and rediscovery of, the higher levels themselves. The fetal and infantile self does not live in any sort of structure that *itself* is being recaptured.

Elevationists often use, as a counterexample to disprove this statement, the existence of tulkus or reincarnated buddhas: fully enlightened beings who remain conscious through all the stages of bardo, infancy, and childhood. Well of course a fully enlightened being is an exception to the rule; but that is a trivial example, because fully enlightened beings are an exception to every rule.

The point is that the infantile self is not immersed in any sort of nirvikalpa or nirvana beyond all suffering and pain and decay; it lives immersed in samsara, with all its hunger, pain, passing pleasure, intense screams, and occasional smiles—but it carries with it, buried in its bosom, the higher levels of its own potential evolution (and the higher states of subtle and causal consciousness), which it can *permanently* contact and bring into full consciousness *only* when its own development moves from prerational to rational to transrational. But the same is true of the adult; so again, nothing has been lost in that regard.

Of course, any of the lower, *prerational* potentials (e.g., various proto-emotions, prana, emotional-sexual impulses) can *themselves* be repressed during early childhood development, and if that occurs, then, as I have strongly maintained all along, successful therapy usually involves regression in service of the ego (what *One Taste* called "the healing spiral"). Moreover, if this repression is severe, it can slow or even completely cripple higher development into transpersonal and superconscious states.

In that case, there needs to occur a spiraling return to early structures: a regression in service of ego (to recontact and repair the early, prerational trauma), and then a progression in transcendence of ego (having repaired the prerational damage, the self can more easily move from rational to transrational adaptation). Even in this spiral of return-and-transcend, what is being contacted is not itself a higher state, but a lower state badly damaged and in need of repair. The Romantic view is again considerably off the mark.

8. In short, the metaphysical fall is the loss of nirvana, which lands us in a world of samsara (a world of sin and separation and duality as if it were actually apart from Spirit); the psychological fall is a painful awareness of that fact, a painful awareness of sin and separation, a painful awareness that we are living in samsara (but have not yet awakened to nirvana). The metaphysical fall lands us in a world of samsara (or a loss of conscious union with Spirit, a loss of nirvana as our realized condition); the psychological fall is an awakening to how painful the world of samsara is (yet before we have rediscovered nirvana or our conscious union with Spirit). Both falls are reversed by spiritual awakening, or a conscious realization of oneness with Spirit, a conscious realization of nirvana. The Romantics confuse not being aware of the pain of samsara with nirvana.

9. According to Christianity, for example, all humans are born in original sin; according to Buddhism, if you are born, it is because you are still karmically slave to the cycle of birth-and-death (samsara), so the very fact you are conceived and born shows that you are not enlightened (unless, again, you are a realized bodhisattva). You are born unenlightened: no part of infancy is an enlightened state, conscious or unconscious, that is then lost. The Romantics, again, have confused the two Falls.

10. Rather, as we saw, and as the wisdom traditions unanimously agree, the real metaphysical fall represents a falling away from awareness of oneness with Spirit, not an actual falling away from Spirit itself (for nothing can exist if divorced from the Ground of All Being). According to the Romantic view, the infant is one with Ground but in an *unconscious* fashion, which is, in fact, quite true; but which actually means that the metaphysical fall has *already* happened with the infant (because it is already *not* conscious of its ever-present union with Ground, as the Romantics themselves agree). The infantile self cannot then *also* break its actual union with the Ground or it would evaporate, and yet that is what the Romantics mistakenly claim is supposed to happen when the infant moves away from its early state—whereas what is actually happening is that, as the infant wakes up to its painful, finite, separate existence, the infant is simply moving into the psychological fall, which the Romantics then perfectly confuse with the metaphysical fall.

11. See Sidebar G, "States and Stages," http://wilber.shambhala.com, on ways that higher states can be ranked in terms of depth of access. With the demise of transpersonal psychology (represented by, e.g., Cortright, Tarnas, Ferrer, Puhakka), these types of judgments become important in terms of how to implement them fairly and impartially. For the passing of transpersonal psychology, see Excerpt F, "Participatory Samsara," as well as Appendix C, "The Death of Psychology and the Birth of the Integral," in "A Summary of My Psychological Model," both posted on

http://wilber.shambhala.com. A summary of the demise of transpersonal psychology is also given by Frances Vaughan on www.integralnaked.org and is highly recommended.

12. Here is the integral theory of evolution and enlightenment (i.e., a theory of enlightenment that still acknowledges evolution). Let's use, for the sake of argument, somebody who was fully enlightened around, let's say, twenty thousand years ago. At that time, the average cultural center of gravity was magical-foraging (preconventional, purple and red meme, egocentric-to-early-ethnocentric, etc.); a few highly evolved souls had pushed into mythic-membership (blue meme). Now, according to this integral theory, in order to be "fully enlightened" at that time, a person's consciousness had to be one with the entire manifest realm or manifest universe. The manifest universe *at that time* included all the nonhuman structures, plus beige, purple, red, and blue. Therefore, if in one's own spiritual development, one had pushed into conscious access of waking, dreaming, deep sleep, and nondual states, *and* one's structural development was at the blue stage/structure, there was literally nothing else in the manifest realm that one could identify with. A person who had done that was literally one with everything that was arising (or could arise at the time). Therefore, that person did indeed possess full unity consciousness, or was as "enlightened" as enlightened could be. On the other hand, somebody who had conscious access to all four major states (waking, dreaming, sleeping, and nondual), but whose center of gravity was purple, would *not* be one with the entire manifest world, because "above his head" would be red and blue structures of consciousness that this person had not transcended-and-included, and had not therefore fully identified with and let go (transcended-and-included). Therefore, such individuals, although they would have access to a variety of states of consciousness, would not be fully enlightened.

Jump forward to today's world, where the average mode is around blue-to-orange, and the leading edge of structural development is, say, right around mature vision-logic (turquoise, meta-paradigmatic). In order to be one with the entire manifest universe, one would again have to have access to the four major states, but one's structural development would now have to be at turquoise, because anything less than that and there would be structures in the universe that were "over one's head." Even if somebody at, say, green, had full access to all major states, there would still be parts of the manifest universe that they had not yet become one with (namely, yellow and turquoise), and therefore they would not be as enlightened as they could be in today's world.

The great advantage of this integral theory is that it lets shamans, saints, and sages living fifty thousand years ago, or ten thousand years ago, or two thousand years ago, be fully enlightened by the criterion of being *one with the entire manifest universe as it existed at that time.* But as evolution moved on, and as more structures and stages emerged (blue, then orange, then green, then yellow, then turquoise), then in order to be one with the entire manifest universe, you must be one with those newly emerged structures as well, which means that in today's world you must be at turquoise (give or take), in order to be in full unity consciousness (sahaj, nondual, permanent one taste). Somebody in today's world could be at, say, mythic-membership (blue), and have full access to meditative or shamanic states, but they would be much less than enlightened.

As I said, there is no other theory that can account for the seemingly paradoxical facts that a person could be fully enlightened yesterday and yet, with the same accomplishment, not fully enlightened today. That doesn't mean this theory is correct, only that at this time it has no competitors that can explain the data. I have run this theory past several dozen other spiritual teachers, and so far all have agreed with its general contours.

This theory itself depends on the post-metaphysical nature of the structures of consciousness as described in volume 2 of the Kosmos trilogy (see excerpts from this at http://wilber.shambhala.com), or the so-called "wilber-5" model. The metaphysical approach to structures/levels of consciousness—found in everything from the Great Chain to Rudolf Steiner to Theosophy to Aurobindo—cannot handle the data, because if there are independently preexisting ontological structures or levels of being/consciousness/bliss, then a person would have to be one with all of those structures or not be enlightened. Since those preexisting structures would be the same a thousand years ago as today, then the requirements for enlightenment would be identical twenty thousand years ago—which is exactly the approach that does *not* work.

Even if you try to prop up the old metaphysical approach by having the structures unfold in an evolutionary fashion, as Aurobindo does, you still have not solved the problem of how somebody with the same consciousness could be enlightened yesterday but not today; and further, you are faced with a new (and intractable) problem: because you maintain that the levels of being/consciousness/bliss are pregiven and preexisting, then how do you know that there aren't even higher preexisting structures beyond your own enlightenment (in which case you cannot be said to be fully enlightened, either)?

All of those problems are inextricably embedded in the old metaphysical approach to enlightenment. Because earlier shamans, saints, and sages were not accessing some of the structures of consciousness that are available today, then by the old metaphysical approach, they couldn't have been deeply enlightened in any meaningful sense. But with a post-metaphysical approach, somebody like Gautama Buddha or Christ could be fully enlightened at their own time, because they were fully one with everything that existed at their time. But in today's world, other structures have evolved that one must now also be one with. But in the metaphysical approach, all the structures are eternally given; to be enlightened, then, one must, even fifty thousand years ago, be one with all of those eternal, archetypally pregiven structures, which no shaman, saint, or sage was—a theory that would consign them all to ignorance. This is unacceptable.

All of those problems are (dis)solved with the post-metaphysical approach of an integral methodological pluralism, which supports an Integral Post-Metaphysics. Keep in mind that a great metaphysician (in the old sense), such as Plotinus or Aurobindo, was still doing nothing but interpreting his or her experiences, including especially his or her spiritual experiences. The metaphysical approach was a natural way to interpret spiritual experiences for those great philosopher-sages. Plotinus, for example, would maintain that there are around a dozen major levels of being/consciousness/bliss. But that is simply an interpretation that he gave to his experiences. He was not out walking around one day and stumbled onto an archetypal building with twelve eternally fixed floors in it. Rather, he had a series of experiences that he interpreted as containing twelve levels or stages—but those are still merely *interpretations* of his direct experiences. But the mythic-membership (blue meme) cultural background in which Plotinus was writing would readily offer metaphysical schemes (with eternally fixed archetypes, unchanging structures, and fixed levels of being and consciousness) as the best way to interpret such experiences, and one cannot fault Plotinus for using the only culture he had. But that does not mean that the only way we can honor Plotinus is by buying into that cultural scheme. Plotinus can be fully respected with a post-metaphysical approach that honors the spirit of Plotinus but finds a different letter.

Similarly with Aurobindo, who was the last, and probably the greatest, of all the great metaphysicians. Aurobindo, too, was simply giving a series of interpretations to his spiritual experiences, but drawing this time on a cultural background that including the German Idealists along with the Vedic traditions. The result was an essentially similar (and still deeply metaphysical) Great Chain of Being/Consciousness/Bliss, but this time the Great Chain unfolded in evolutionary time. But it otherwise has all the problems associated with the metaphysical approach that Aurobindo still inhabits, including preexisting ontological structures, pregiven realities untouched by cultural intersubjectivity, realms inhabited by beings essentially context-transcending in all modes of knowing, and so on. In other words, all the old metaphysical assumptions that cannot survive the valid moments of criticism offered by Kantian and postmodern epistemologies. Aurobindo was perhaps the last and the greatest of the metaphysicians, standing on the brink of the post-metaphysical age but unable to enter.

(There are still many times that I continue to use the word "metaphysics," since it conveys a certain set of ideas, and I cannot always be explaining why my approach is post-metaphysical. Context will have to determine, in each case, what sense is being conveyed.)

Were, then, any of the original shamans enlightened by these post-metaphysical standards? If they were, they would have to have had (1) conscious access to (at least) the four major states of consciousness present (waking/grosss, dreaming/subtle, formless/causal, and ever-present/nondual), and (2) a frontal structure at blue. I believe that there were at least some shamans who met these criteria; and thus, stretching back to perhaps 50,000 B.C.E. or more, there were enlightened human beings (as enlightened as enlightened could be at those times, inasmuch as they were one with the entire manifest universe as it existed at that point in evolution).

But as discussed in the main text, those shamans appear to be the exception, because the typical shamanic voyage did not master the causal (nor therefore, the true nondual). Further, even if it did (and to focus on the frontal structure), in today's world, those who were one with no higher than blue would be ethnocentric in the worst sense. For all those reasons, although we can clearly recognize enlightened exceptions, the typical shamanic path was not fully enlightened, even by our very generous (least demanding) definition of enlightenment or awakening.

13. There is a difference between be able to inflict damage on nature using technologically sophisticated but damaging modes (such as coal-burning steam engines) and yet consciously choosing not to inflict that damage (which would indeed be ecological wisdom) versus not being able to inflict any damage in the first place because one hasn't those sophisticated means to do so. Much of the ecological wisdom ascribed to early tribes was of the latter variety—that is, lack of means should not be confused with presence of wisdom. Worse, even with limited means, they managed to inflict a relatively huge amount of ecological damage, as Crichton points out.

14. What about the final claim of certain sophisticated Romantics? Namely, that even if the magical structure is a less developed structure of consciousness (predifferentiated and not transdifferentiated), nonetheless a truly integral structure would result if the naturic wholeness of the magical structure were combined with the rational structure of modernity. I agree that would be a welcome integration, but it would simply be an integration of prerational and rational; it would *not* be transrational. Moreover, the magical structure itself is not the only structure other than rationality that is supposed to be included in the integration: there are the entire realms of mythic-horticultural and mythic-rational-agrarian, all of which Romantic-tribalists generally despise. Finally, even if we toss in the most advanced mode (shamanism), this is, as we saw, a partial and limited approach to the overall transpersonal. From almost any angle, the foraging structure simply cannot perform the herculean feats the Romantics demand of it, but rather remains a very important but very limited mode.

15. In addition to translation and transformation, *A Sociable God* discusses transcription. Transcription is not a term I often use anymore, but its general point is still valid. Relativists rather despised the concept, because they felt that it meant that the basic structures were given, and thus all cultures were consigned to merely reading (transcribing) a fixed set of pregiven options. Transcription was never meant in anything like that rigid a conception, but never mind; in the post-metaphysical approach of phase-5, it is even less confining. Transcription simply means that a specific occasion will tend to arise within a particular probability space (this probability space is what is crudely meant by "structure" in the metaphysical traditions). Still, as I said, I don't use that term very much because critics have an especially hard time understanding it adequately.

16. We saw that if the metaphysical fall means anything, it means, not a loss of being one with the Ground, since by definition all things are one with Ground or they would cease to exist; but rather, it means a *loss of our awareness of our oneness with Spirit or Ground.* But according to even the Romantics, the early infant and the early dawn humans were "one with Ground but in an unconscious fashion," which means the metaphysical fall had *already* occurred, which indeed it had, which is why dawn humans and infants are *already* "born in sin" or born into a world of samsara, separation, finitude, and death. The infant does not escape finitude, hunger, or pain, only its awareness of its finitude! Hence, the infant—and dawn human—are already existing in a metaphysically fallen state—a state of samsara, sin, finitude, and death—but they are not yet fully and painfully aware of it—that is, the metaphysical fall has occurred but not yet the psychological fall.

The Romantics, as we saw, simply confused these two falls, and thus were forced to depict the infantile dawn state as a state that existed in a historical time (ontogenetically, right around birth, and phylogenetically, around a million years ago) that was before both the metaphysical fall and the psychological fall, and thus were forced to read into the historical infantile state some sort of spiritual purity on earth, some sort of actual presence of nirvana (instead of a simple lack of awareness of samsara). The actual or real metaphysical fall occurs *prior* to manifestation and prior to evolution (and is often called involution); the psychological fall occurs *during* manifestation or during evolution, at the point that humans *become conscious* of their fallen nature, or *become aware* that they are not consciously one with Spirit or Ground. The metaphysical fall is the creation of a world that apparently (or illusorily) exists apart from Spirit; the psychological fall is becoming aware of the metaphysical fall. Both are healed by a conscious realization of nondual Spirit.

The real disaster of this approach is then that the steps out of this immersion in samsara are condemned as a metaphysical fall, whereas they are the first necessary steps in reversing that fall. Hence, the regressive nature of so much of Romanticism, and its inadvertent slide into the disease that it calls the cure.

17. It was *Sex, Ecology, Spirituality* that first specifically laid out the correlations of the Lower-Left quadrant (archaic, magic, mythic, rational, vision-logic) and the Lower-Right quadrant (foraging, horticultural, agrarian, industrial, informational) and further correlated those quadrants with the others. *A Sociable God* did not specifically discuss the Lower-Right quadrant, and *Up from Eden* tended to treat Lower-Left and Lower-Right as one dimension. It would be in phase-4 that these various distinctions and correlations were made. But *A Sociable God* and *Up from Eden* laid a foundation by correlating Upper Left and Lower Left in terms of a specific analysis of levels of structural organization and relational exchange.

18. For an elucidation of the new Person-Centered Civil Religion, with its panenhenic outlook, see *One Taste*, September 23 entry.

19. Well, in any event, I first presented that phase-3 model in "Ontogenetic Development: Two Fundamental Patterns" (*Journal of Transpersonal Psychology*, 1981), which appeared in *Eye to Eye* as "Structure, Stage, and Self" (included in volume 3 of the *Collected Works*). The "two patterns" in the original title referred to the difference between the enduring basic structures (the major levels or waves in the spectrum of consciousness), and the transitional lines or streams that make their way through the basic levels. This understanding was implicit even in *The Atman Project*, where on several occasions I stated that "although I have placed side-by-side such items as cognitive development, moral development, and ego development, I do not at all mean to equate them. . . . Loevinger, for one, thinks ego development is independent of psychosexual development. Kohlberg has shown that intellectual [cognitive] development is necessary but not sufficient for moral development. And so it goes, with all sorts of various developmental threads [developmental lines] running parallel, independent, and/or correlative with all sorts of other developmental threads." That was written in 1978, during phase-2; but by 1981, with phase-3, I made all of those distinctions very explicit, and began to carefully present these different threads as the relatively independent streams that they are, while also

continuing to emphasize the universal nature of the general waves in the overall spectrum of consciousness itself.

This move to phase-3 invalidated very few of the actual propositions of phase-2; it simply set them in a larger context. The pre/trans fallacy, for example, still applied to any developmental sequence, but it was now understood that there are many such sequences, so that a person could be preconventional in one line, conventional in another, and postconventional in yet another. The pre/trans fallacy was still valid, but one had to be sure one had a single developmental line each time one applied it. This changed none of the conclusions of phase-2, but opened them up to even richer elaborations.

Prologue

THIS BOOK IS an introductory overview of the psychology and sociology of religion, with particular emphasis on how modern sociological theory might benefit from a dialogue with the perennial philosophy—that is, from transcendental or "transpersonal" perspectives (hence the subtitle). In the terms of current sociology, it is an introduction to a "nonreductionistic" sociology of religion (or worldviews in general), and it is based on various tenets taken from modern functionalism (e.g., Parsons), hermeneutics (e.g., Gadamer), and developmental-structuralism (e.g., Habermas), all of which are carefully set in a context of transcendental or transpersonal possibilities (e.g., William James). The book is not "merely metaphysical" or "hopelessly idealistic," however, for it contains concrete methodologies and strategies for hypothesis formation and testing.

Of course, a transcendental or transpersonal sociology is, in part, a new type of approach; nonetheless, its topic is of direct and immediate relevance to any number of current social, psychological, and religious theories and topics, including the new religious movements in America, cults, the influx of Eastern mystical traditions, the breakdown of "civil religion," the psychology of religious experience, meditation, the process of sociological "legitimation" of worldviews, humanistic and transpersonal psychology, moral development, and so on—all of which, more or less, are woven together in the following pages by virtue of the scope of the topic itself. Scholars as well as educated laypersons concerned with any of those topics might thus find the book of interest.

I have, then, tried to provide the briefest possible statement of, and introduction to, a general transcendental sociology. *Brief,* for several reasons. For one, this is, in part, and as far as I know, the first attempt to broach the transcendental aspects of the subject, and first attempts deserve brevity. For another, I wished this book to be a concise statement of the *possibilities* of this field and not a rambling dissertation on its necessary content. The book itself, although scholarly, is meant to be accessible to the educated layperson interested in psychology, sociology, and religion, and brevity makes it that much more accessible. For scholars in these fields, my presentation of "just the skeleton" will allow them to add the meat and flesh of their own ideas, perspectives, and insights, without any further interference from me, thus arriving at a variety of fleshed-out products by virtue of their own additions (coproductions, as it were). I believe this skeleton is sound enough, and new enough, that no more need be presented in this initial outing; to do so would simply run the risk of overdetermining a new and fragile topic. Finally, by keeping the account sparse, I felt that the volume might more easily be used as an auxiliary text or for outside reading in any number of college or graduate courses on closely related topics.

But because this *is* a short introductory presentation, I have occasionally had to state my suggestions in a rather dogmatic and conclusive fashion. I would therefore like to emphasize that the following suggestions are, in fact, offered as hypotheses, and hypotheses that can potentially be tested—and potentially rejected—by a set of experimental methodologies. These methodologies are outlined in the last chapter. I might also say that this is one of those slightly awkward topics whose individual parts can better be understood once the overall topic is itself grasped, and thus this is one of those books that benefit from a second reading. At the least, the reader might, at the end, briefly reflect on the points that went before and see if they do not make a type of comprehensive sense perhaps not obvious at the first reading.

The word "transpersonal" might be new to some readers. For the moment, suffice it to say that it involves, in part, a sustained and experimental *inquiry* into spiritual, or transcendental (transpersonal), or "perennial philosophical" concerns. And it does so *not* in order to uncritically validate all so-called "religious experiences" but to attempt to develop legitimate and reproducible means for differentiating between authentic spiritual experience, if such indeed exists, and merely psychotic, hallucinatory, grandiose-exhibitionistic, paranoid, delusional, or other abnormal or pathological states. It is a *critical* discipline.

But because this book is, in part, one of the first attempts to bring a transpersonal or critical-transcendental dimension to sociology, it is faced with both a blessing and a curse. Blessing, in that one may, with only a modicum of intelligence, make pioneering observations, by simple definition. Curse, in that there are no precedents against which to judge the real value of those observations. This is quite different from even the recently introduced field of transpersonal psychology, for transpersonal psychology—under different names—actually goes all the way back to Plato, Augustine, and Plotinus, in the West, and Buddhaghosa, Patanjali, and Asanga in the East, and it can claim such contributors as Kant, Hegel, Bradley, Eckhart, C. G. Jung, William James, Jaspers, et al. This is because psychology itself, as a distinct discipline, goes back at least to Aristotle's *De Anima*, and transpersonal psychology, by whatever name, is simply the approach to psychology from the perspectives of the *philosophia perennis*, an approach that is thus as old as the perennial philosophy itself. Under the title "transpersonal psychology" it is, in a sense, a new and modern discipline, but it has a very old and very honorable history.

Sociology, on the other hand, is counted as perhaps the youngest of all the human sciences. Certain Renaissance and Enlightenment scholars—Hobbes, Locke, Rousseau, Machiavelli, Montesquieu, Vico—were sociologists of a sort. But it was not really until the nineteenth century, when the concept of *society* was finally distinguished from that of the *state*, that sociology emerged as a distinct discipline. The term "sociology" itself was not coined until 1838, by Auguste Comte, and its two great "founders," Émile Durkheim and Max Weber, wrote their first pioneering works in 1893 and 1920, respectively. A mere several decades ago.

Here is the catch: sociology, yet an infant, arose in an intellectual climate largely dominated by the then-fashionable scientific materialism, and many of its early proponents were overly influenced by mechanistic science (e.g., Comte) or material interactions (e.g., Marx), with the result that their sociologies are expressly reductionistic. Even that sensitive scholar Durkheim has recently been labeled, by Robert Bellah, as one of the two "great reductionists" in human sciences (the other being Freud). Being such a young science, sociology has only recently moved to correct these reductionistic trends, by, among other things, using models based on living and not mechanical systems (e.g., Parsonian functionalism) and introducing phenomenology and interpretive disciplines, or the study of the *meaning* of mental acts *as* mental acts and not merely as reducible to empirical-objective behaviorisms (Schutz, Berger, etc.).

All of that is good news, and all of that will be touched upon in the following pages. Beyond that, however, sociology has still not been opened to those concerns embodied in the perennial philosophy. On the one hand, this is because sociology is indeed an infant; it had not the advantage of being exposed to a Plato, a Spinoza, a Hegel, a Leibniz—all perennial philosophers of a sort. On the other hand, it is only recently that a modern, *experimental,* and systematic inquiry into the essential tenets of the *philosophia perennis* has been undertaken (largely by transpersonal psychologists), and so, prior to this, just exactly how to infuse sociology with genuinely transcendental or transpersonal concerns might not have been all that apparent anyway. In any event, I believe the time is now ripe for such an infusion.

The point is that the modern psychology of religion ought to have something to offer the modern sociology of religion, and this book is a short introduction to both.

1

The Background Problem
vis-à-vis Religion

T HE AIM OF THIS BOOK is to suggest some contributions that transpersonal psychology might be able to make to the science of sociology, and especially the sociology of religion, by, first, sketching out the basics of transpersonal psychology and, second, transposing these basics into the categories and dimensions of modern sociological theory. That done, specific topics and problems—such as the new religions, cognitive validity of religious knowledge, some definitions of religion itself, hermeneutics and structuralism in religious universals, methodology of religious inquiry, and so forth—will be broached. It should be emphasized, however, that because of the large amount of theoretical ground that has to be covered quickly, this presentation will necessarily take place on a very tentative, generalized, and informal level.

The initial problem, for both the psychology and sociology of religion, is to provide theories and methodologies for determining or understanding the purpose, and perhaps secondarily the validity, of religious involvement. I would like very briefly to review the major sociological (and orthodox psychological) responses to this problem, in order to highlight the areas to which transpersonal psychology might eventually contribute.

PRIMITIVIZATION THEORY

One of the first and apparently reflex approaches is "primitivization," which views religion in general as the product of lower or primitive stages of human development or evolution. In sociology, for example, Comte's famous "law of three" sees historical evolution as moving from myth-religion to metaphysics to rational science, in which case religion is simply viewed as a primitive consolation for a primitive mentality. Transposed by modern developmental psychologists, this phylogenetic development seems to find many parallels in today's ontogenetic development: the infant goes from prototaxic magical thinking to parataxic mythical thinking to syntaxic rationality.[87] Religion, it again seems, is prompted by fixations or regressions to infantile magic or childish myth, the latter being particularly marked by Oedipal object-relations and thus susceptible to paternal or especially patriarchal introjections and subsequent projections as a heavenly Father,[29] now loving, now vengeful, now jealous, now forgiving—everything you ever wanted to know about Jehovah. From primitivization sociology to rational-emotive theory to psychoanalysis to orthodox cognitive psychology, this "religious = childish" formalization has been pandemic, with Freud himself *(The Future of an Illusion)* leading the way.[31] Piaget also has extensively traced out the magical, mythical, "religious-type" thinking of early childhood and documented how such thinking tends to drop out as more formal and rational modes of thought emerge and develop.[70]

That particular developmental sequence—magic to myth to rationality—is not to be denied, as we will soon see in detail; problematic is its capacity to explain all, or even most, of the essential contours of religion. To give only the mildest objection now: even if all religious involvements were indicative of infantile-childish cognitions, that would at best explain their source but not their function or purpose—their *meaning* for those subscribing to them and their function in society at large.

FUNCTIONALISM

It is not uncommon, then, that if a sensitive scholar first embraces primitivization as explanatory, he or she eventually moves on to some sort of functionalist approach (e.g., Parsons, Merton, Luhmann), if not to completely replace primitivization, then at least to supplement it.[62, 69] In functionalism or general systems theory, groups or societies are viewed as organic systems, with each of their "parts" (religion, education, customs, etc.) serving some type of potentially useful or necessary function. Religious symbolism is thus analyzed in terms of the salutary functions it serves in such specific areas as pattern maintenance, tension reduction, goal attainment, and so forth of the overall social organism. From this view, religious symbolism, if indeed it functions adequately (i.e., if it helps the system to reproduce itself), is to that extent *appropriate*.

In general functionalism, the functions and meanings of group or social activities are often divided into two dimensions, manifest and latent. The manifest function has a recognized value—it is more or less conscious, explicit, and expressed. The latent function, on the other hand, is neither recognized nor consciously intended—it is more or less implicit and unexpressed. Merton,[62] who introduced this distinction in sociology (cf. Freud's similar distinction in dreams), used the Hopi rain dance as an example. The manifest function of the ritual is to bring rain. However, such rituals also "fulfill the latent function of reinforcing the group identity by providing a periodic occasion on which the scattered members of a group assemble to engage in a common activity." The manifest meaning is apparent to the members of the group; the latent meaning, however, can usually be discovered only by specific functional analysis, that is, by the attempt to determine what the empirical and *objective* function of a particular relationship actually is and does, despite what the subscribers say or think it does (the manifest and subjective explanation).

When it comes to religion, then, various rites, symbols, and beliefs can be seen as serving legitimate functions. For even if, on a manifest level, the religious symbols are not objectively "true" (e.g., even if the rain dance does not actually bring rain), nonetheless on a latent level the rites and symbols serve a very necessary, useful, and to that extent "true" function: they help preserve and protect the overall integrity and cohesion of the group (they help the system to reproduce itself). Thus religious symbols, whether or not "objectively true," can nonetheless serve a legitimate purpose in the self-regulating social system. In short, religion serves some sort of function, perhaps hidden, and therefore has some sort of meaning, perhaps latent, in a given group or culture.

This, of course, is very similar to aspects of pragmatic psychology, such as that proposed by William James. Religious symbols can be appropriate units in the functioning of the psyche, regardless of the "objective truth value" of their supposed referents. For James, the very *belief* in spiritual realities could serve a salutary purpose that itself validated—indeed constituted—the truth-claim of the belief.[51]

There is clearly merit to this approach, and we will want to retain aspects of it in our overall formulation (even as we will find a place for a type of limited primitivization). But the functionalist approach in and by itself is expressly reductionistic. Religion is not actually a communion with some sort of true divinity, spirit, or godhead; it is really not much more than a safety-valve function. Its referent is not actual divinity; its *referent* is merely other symbols in a circle of social transactions. In other words, religion is not really religious; it is not about very God, but about various god-symbols, themselves composed of merely human social reciprocities.

If used exclusively, this approach heavy-handedly negates or at least re-interprets the actual validity claims of the subscribers themselves, and thus bypasses or reduces the central part, the subjective part, the phenomena it is asked to explain. Not surprisingly, it is forced to place the "real meaning" of religiousness exclusively in a latent dimension where it can hide from the objections of the subscribers. This is not to deny that there *are* latent dimensions and functions in a belief system, for there are; it is to object to the pandemic reduction of the manifest-subjective intentionality to a latent-empirical function.

Thus, for functionalism, Lao Tzu, Buddha, Krishna, and Christ were not really intuiting a transcendent ground of being, which is what *they* said they were doing (their manifest intent). The functionalist can find no objective evidence, no empirical referent, for this "transcendental ground," and therefore what these sages were *really* doing was serving some sort of merely latent function unknown to them. The transcendental ground, *as* transcendental ground, never enters the picture, contrary to everything the sages themselves actually had to say on the subject.

But there are orthodox objections to exclusive functionalist systems theory as well. Preeminent among them is the apparent fact that human goal states and values cannot be determined via empirical-analytic or merely objective methods.[32] For, unlike the merely biological systems that form the basis of the functionalist model, human interactions also possess conscious meanings, values, goals, and purposes, and these relations are not so much objective as they are intersubjective. Consequently, they are disclosed not so much by objective measurement and analysis as by intersubjective communication and interpretation, and these intersubjective interpretations slide through the system without leaving completely empirical-objective footprints.[38] For example, one cannot easily devise an empirical-scientific test that will disclose the meaning of *Hamlet*. *Hamlet* is a mental and symbolic production whose meanings and values disclose themselves only in a community of inter-subjective interpreters. Functionalism, in its attempt to be empirical and objective, often misses the essence of these intersubjective meanings and values. On the other hand, if one attempts to overcome this shortcoming by simply stipulating the goal values and states that will then guide anal-ysis of the system, that amounts to a normative and interpretive as op-posed to empirical approach, which functionalism claims to be. Trying to account for these normative-interpretive dimensions by feeding them back into the empirical functions of the system (e.g., Luhmann) is again to reduce the former to the latter.

PHENOMENOLOGICAL-HERMENEUTICS

As theorist-researchers begin to question this reductionism (in its psy-chological or sociological forms), it is not uncommon for them to move from exclusively functionalist analyses to something resembling phe-nomenological-hermeneutics: from at least one completely valid per-spective, *the religious symbol is exactly what it says it is*. It is not merely a manifest function hiding the real latent function, or just a safety valve, or only a tension-reduction or social-cohesion mechanism—it is funda-mentally what it says it is. If Buddha or Krishna was lucid and legitimate in his communicative meaning, and he said he was contacting a funda-mental ground of being, then that is our only starting point. And if I want to *understand* that point, if I want to understand anyone else's symbols and meanings, then the best approach is some sort of *empa-thetic interpretation* (just as if I wished to understand *Hamlet* or any other symbolic communication). I must *reproduce* in *my* awareness via *interpretation* the *inner* world or meaning of Krishna or Hamlet or Job or whomever, there only to grasp its essential message.[32,49,46,68]

The science of such interpretation is generally called "hermeneutics," from the Greek *hermeneutikos,* to translate or interpret, and from Hermes, god of science, commerce, and eloquence. Hermeneutics has its modern roots in general phenomenology, or the attempt to discover the nature and meaning of mental acts *as* mental acts, and not merely as reduced to various objective, sensory, and empirical displays. For a merely sensory-empirical object—say a rock—does not necessarily point to or refer to anything other than itself. But a *mental* event—a concept or symbol—by its very nature points to or *refers to* other entities and events, including *other* symbols, which themselves can refer to yet other symbols, and so on in an *intersubjective* circle of symbolic meanings and values. In short, a mental act *as* mental act is what Husserl called *intentional:* it has *meaning* or *value* because it refers to or embraces other occasions, including other meanings and symbols and values. Phenomenology is an attempt to directly study this realm of intersubjective *intelligibilia,* not merely the realm of objective *sensibilia,* and hermeneutics is simply the branch of phenomenology that is especially concerned with interpreting the meanings of these intersubjective or intentional symbols.

Accordingly, if I want to understand the meaning of a particular religious system, I must not do so in a merely empirical, objective, reductionistic fashion. I must first empathetically understand the system by reproducing or entering its intersubjective and interpretive circle (the "hermeneutic circle"). Schools differ as to whether interpretation should be empathetic or actually participant (where feasible), but some form of *inside understanding* and *interpretive engagement* is deemed absolutely fundamental. The *meaning* of a religious expression is not solely or even especially to be found in, for example, its latent tension management, but rather in its manifest intentionality and its intersubjective acknowledgment. And the way you—as an "outside investigator"—determine that intersubjective meaning is to enter (not necessarily physically) the hermeneutic circle itself, the circle constituted by the intersubjective exchange of linguistic symbols, an exchange that is always set in a particular *historical* context. Hence the common title: historical-hermeneutics. If I want to understand the religious meaning of the word "sin," for example, I must take into account the *historical* context of the symbol itself, because what is "sin" to one epoch is not necessarily "sin" to another (whatever happened to gluttony and sloth, once "deadly sins"?). Merely defining "sin" objectively misses its historical referents and thus leads to bad interpretations, bad hermeneutics, ethnocentric bias, and so forth.[33,34]

This general phenomenological-hermeneutical approach has had an immense influence on both the psychology of religion—James's *Varieties* is a type of forerunner—and the sociology of religion—Ricoeur, for example, or Robert Bellah's "symbolic realism," which is a type of hermeneutic Durkheim, if I am allowed to say that. Likewise, I have watched many psychologist colleagues move from an initial fascination with systems theory and psychocybernetics (the scurrying of information bits through personless neurons) to a more comprehensive system that also includes an attempt to grasp the *meaning* of that information in terms of a self that shapes and is shaped by history. The self as history, hopelessly interlocked with other selves as history, constitutes not merely information but a *story,* a *text,* with beginnings and middles and endings and ups and downs and outcomes, and the way you grasp the meaning of a text is via good interpretation: hermeneutics.

There is obviously much to be said for phenomenological-hermeneutics, and we will be drawing significantly on many of its tenets as we proceed. But taken in and by itself, hermeneutics seems finally to suffer a series of unhappy limitations. Foremost among these is its radicalization of situational truth and its consequent lack of a universal or even quasi-universal critical dimension, a way to judge the actual validity, not just interpretive mesh, of a religious truth claim. Krishna may have been transcending, but was the Hopi really producing rain? How are we to differentiate the authentic from the less than authentic engagements? Hermeneutics of course denies that such a critical or universal dimension exists, thereby relativizing all cultural truths with the quite illogical exception of its own claim that such is always (i.e., universally) the case.

For hermeneutics, all religious expressions—indeed, all symbolic productions—are to be understood from the inside; *verstehenden* sociology at its extreme. If you are *in* the hermeneutic circle, consensual interpretive agreement is validation; if you are outside the circle, you are not allowed a judgment. In neither case can the circle itself be shown to be wrong, or partially wrong, or even just *partial.* Such theoretical absolutizing of cultural relativity often translates itself, in the field, into exasperation,[3] an exasperation apparently due in some cases, not to incorrect methodological application, but to a more native preunderstanding that not *all* religious expressions are "true" and that some form of critical appraisal is mandatory.

Hermeneuticists and symbolic realists, of course, reply that this exasperation must be due to methodological or interpretive malfunction, because there is no *external standard* against which religious expressions could possibly be critically appraised, without, it is said, committing reductionism. Thus, any attempt to say other than what the particular hermeneutic circle itself says is, in a priori fashion, charged with reductionism, and thus hermeneutics, in and by itself, under the guise that it is being "nonreductionistic," tends all too rapidly to slide into the limp notion that "*all* religions are true," a stance that precludes any sort of sustained critical appraisal. Hermeneutics has no teeth.

DEVELOPMENTAL STRUCTURALISM

Not only does exclusive hermeneutics deny those truths of functionalist systems theory that *are* partially true—for example, the possibility that there are latent functions performed by a text outside the knowledge of the text—it also overlooks the advances made in modern structural-developmental sciences, especially in the lines of Baldwin,[8] Piaget,[70] Werner,[95] Kohlberg,[54] and Loevinger.[57] For the seminal discovery of these disciplines is that psychological structures develop in a *hierarchic* fashion. Barring arrest, regression, or fixation, each stage of development includes, comprehends, or subsumes the basic elements of its predecessors but adds significant structures and functions not found in its predecessors—each stage "transcends and includes" its predecessors in a *nested hierarchy,* a development that is envelopment.[100] The senior level includes the junior but *not vice versa,* and it is that "not vice versa" that constitutes and establishes a very real hierarchy. Each senior stage displays a greater degree of structuralization, differentiation-integration, organization, functional capacity, and so on through a dozen variables found to define, via a developmental-logic, the meaning of the word *higher.* Thus, developmental psychologists speak unabashedly about *higher stages* of cognition (Piaget), ego development (Loevinger), interpersonal relations (Selman), moralization (Kohlberg), and even *quality,* as the psychoanalyst Rapaport explains: "*Structures are hierarchically ordered.* This assumption is significant because it is the foundation for the psychoanalytic propositions concerning differentiation . . . , and because it implies that the *quality of a process depends upon the level of the structural hierarchy on which it takes place*"[76] (my italics).

Accepting for the moment that psychology is always also social psychology, this overall hierarchization is extremely significant, because it apparently gives us—perhaps for the first time—a paradigm to *adjudicate the comparative degree of validity* of various psychosocial productions (including religious expressions). A similar approach has already been suggested by Habermas,[41] who wants to use, among other schemes, Kohlberg's stage-structures of moralization to adjudicate the developmental level of interactive competence evidenced in various individuals and, indeed, societies and historical epochs at large.

Before looking more carefully at this nested hierarchy paradigm, let us note that Habermas explicitly recognizes it as a corrective to historical-hermeneutic inquiry. Habermas utilizes some of the essentials of hermeneutics, such as its emphasis on narrative history and communicative competence, but he stresses that against hermeneutics, as a *narrative foil,* must be placed the hierarchic realizations of a developmental-logic. The fact of *levels* of narrative development *imposes* on any given narrative a competency status that is not and cannot be determined solely by empathetic interpretation of the narrative itself. There is, in other words, some sort of *external corrective* to the heremeneutic circle, and that external corrective is a scheme of developmental levels of narrative competence.

Finally, we note that, by virtue of nested hierarchy, each higher structure of consciousness is potentially capable of *legitimately criticizing* the partiality, but not the phase-specific appropriateness, of its lower predecessors, precisely as, for example, a person of formal operational thinking can criticize the lopsided egocentrism of preoperational thinking, or a stage-5 moral stance will criticize the lack of perspectivism of stage-2 stance. In other words, structural-developmentalism seems to give us that universal or quasi-universal critical dimension or external corrective apparently lacking in merely hermeneutic, phenomenological, or symbolic realist approaches.

OUR OVERALL APPROACH

With all of the above as background, we can now state that the crux of this book is the suggestion that there exists a nested hierarchy not only of psychosocial development but also of authentic religious development, and that, in fact, these two run precisely into each other as two ends of a single spectrum, and that, finally, the hierarchical nature of this spectrum will give us a critical-normative sociology of religion, one that is capable of *structurally analyzing* various religious expressions, assigning them a spot in the hierarchy, consequently adjudicating their degree of authenticity, and accordingly pronouncing that, in terms of an *overall critical sociological theory,* this or that religious engagement is *higher* than this or that other religious engagement, *precisely* as we now say, for example, a stage-6 moral response is higher than a stage-4 response. In addition to this developmental-structuralism, we will also find necessary, appropriate, but circumscribed roles for functional systems analyses, hermeneutical inquiries, and even a type of primitivization theory, attempting, as it were, to salvage the moments of truth of each of the approaches we have so briefly discussed.

Before we begin such a construction, we need some background information, particularly from the field of transpersonal developmental psychology.

2

The Nested Hierarchy of Structural Organization

THE ORTHODOX BASE

H ERE IS A VERY SIMPLIFIED, streamlined, and composite version of the nested hierarchy of structural organization as discovered by orthodox developmental psychology (I have included a few of their Eastern psychological correlates for future reference).

1. *Physical:* the simple physical substratum of the organism (the first and lowest Buddhist *skandha;* the first and lowest yogic chakra; *annamayakosha* in Vedanta).

2. *Sensoriperceptual:* the areas of sensation (the second skandha) and perception (the third skandha) treated as one general realm; simple sensorimotor cognition (Piaget).

3. *Emotional-sexual:* the sheath of bioenergy, libido, élan vital, or prana (the fourth skandha in Buddhism, the *pranamayakosha* in Vedanta; second chakra).*

4. *Magical:* the beginning of the mental realms; this includes simple images, symbols, and the first rudimentary concepts, or the first and lowest mental productions, which are "magical" in the sense

---

* For simplicity's sake, I will usually refer to these lowest three levels as "the" *archaic* level.

70

that they display condensation, displacement, confusion of image and object, "omnipotence of thought," animism, and so forth. There is also a lack of perspectivism, or an inability to clearly take the role of other. This is Freud's primary process, Arieti's paleologic, Piaget's preoperational thinking (the third chakra). It is correlated with Kohlberg's preconventional morality, Loevinger's impulsive and self-protective stages, Maslow's safety needs, and so forth.

5. *Mythic:* more advanced than magic, with a beginning of concrete operational thinking (Piaget) and a beginning of perspectivism (or communal role-taking), but still incapable of the simplest hypothetico-deductive reasoning, consequently "mythic" in its operation (cf. Gebser); the overall "lower mind" (the fourth chakra, the beginning of *manomayakosha* in Vedanta and *manovijnana* in Mahayana). It is correlated with Loevinger's conformist and conscientious-conformist stages, Maslow's belongingness needs, Kohlberg's conventional morality, and so forth. Because of its overall *conformity* status, we often refer to this general level as "mythic-membership."

6. *Rational:* Piaget's formal operational thinking (the fifth chakra, the culmination of manomayakosha and manovijnana). It is the first structure that can not only think about the world but think about thinking; hence, it is the first structure that is clearly self-reflexive and introspective, and it displays an advanced capacity for perspectivism. It is also the first structure capable of hypothetico-deductive or propositional reasoning ("if a, then b"), which allows it to apprehend higher or purely noetic *relationships*. It is correlated with Loevinger's conscientious and individualistic stages, Kohlberg's post-conventional morality, Maslow's self-esteem needs, and so forth.

Figure 1 (page 44) indicates these general stage-structures and their hierarchical nature. I have placed a gap between each structure to indicate that they are largely emergent or discontinuous in development; that is, they cannot be fully reduced to or explained solely in terms of their predecessor(s)—what has come to be called emergent evolution[71] or milestone development[57] (which does not preclude the continuous and linearly unbroken development *within* each level, or what is known as "polar development"). Each line in figure 1 is evolution; each gap, revolution.

THE TRANSPERSONAL LEVELS

The problem of this section is, Where in figure 1 does religious expression belong?

Let us begin by noting that there is an increasing reacceptance, among developmental-structuralists, of the notion of phylogenetic/ontogenetic parallels: Primitive-paleolithic magic is similar in deep structure (*not* surface structure) to infantile–early childhood preoperational thinking; classic religio-mythic expressions are similar in deep structure to late childhood preoperational and beginning concrete operational thinking; and modern rational-science is top of the hierarchy with adolescent-to-adult formal operational and hypothetico-deductive reasoning.[5,66,95,105] As Arieti[5] explains,

> What is of fundamental importance is that the [two] processes to a large extent follow similar developmental plans. This does not mean literally that in the psyche . . . ontogeny recapitulates phylogeny, but that there are certain similarities in the . . . fields of development and that we are able to individualize schemes of highest forms of generality [deep structures, for example, as in figure 1] which involve all levels of the psyche in its [different] types of development.

If we accept for the moment that there is some sort of truth to that idea—for I think there most definitely is—then we are faced with certain

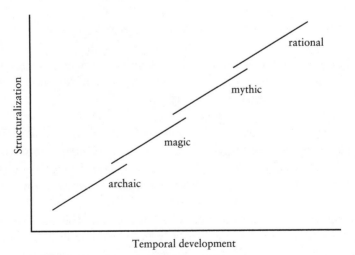

Temporal development

FIGURE 1

grave problems vis-à-vis legitimizing religious consciousness. For what we have, when figure 1 is seen to be not only an ontogenetic but also a phylogenetic/ideogenetic chart, is actually a very sophisticated theory of religious primitivization, an update and slight expansion of Comte's law of three. For, if we treat religion as a structure among other structures, and not something potentially shared by them all (we will investigate that later), then *increasing historical development* clearly shows an eventually *decreasing religiosity.* Paleolithic humans had magic religion: totem ritual that expressed the fusion of human and animal ancestor, voodoo-like rituals, animistic beliefs, and so on. Neolithic and Bronze Age humans had classical mythic religion: gods and goddesses controlling their fate, with petitionary rituals and prayers offered by humans to their heavenly fathers and mothers. And then, finally, comes the revolution of rationality (starting with Greece c. sixth century B.C., reaching its stride with eighteenth-century Enlightenment thought but only today beginning to claim a clearly dominant structural role).[105] This increasing rationalization brought the eventual retreat of religion (in any conventional sense) as a widespread, legitimate worldview, its place being taken increasingly by hypothetico-deductive reasoning, empirical-analytic inquiry, and technical interests, as sociologists from Weber onward have noted.

By this scheme there is no highly developed religious structure of consciousness, for the highest structure is rational-scientific. It appears that we have no choice but to capitulate to the primitivizationists, psychoanalysts, and such—religion is *basically* a primitive fixation/regression to infantile magic or childhood myth (rationalized, if necessary). Such a *developmental argument,* I believe, can even disarm Bellah's refutation of psychoanalytic reductionism, because here the analyst is not interpreting religious symbolism in terms of something foreign to the person himself, but rather is demonstrating that the religious symbol has its own internal structure that *places itself* in the history of hierarchic structuralization of the person's psyche. Analysis merely helps the individual to remember and reconstruct this history so as to more clearly see how it is presently opaque in its influence. To say this is reductionistic is to say that helping a person move from stage-3 morality to stage 4, 5, or 6 is reductionistic.

There are only two ways out of this impasse. The first is to claim that phylogenetic/ideogenetic evolution is in fact devolution—that there actually existed in the past a historical Garden of Eden on earth, perhaps in the Bronze Age of mythic religion, and that we have gone steadily downhill since. Since evolution is really devolution, the *earlier* stages are really *higher*. To empirical scientists this might seem a somewhat silly notion, but I remind the reader that such sober and respected religious scholars as Joseph Campbell[23] and Huston Smith[86] have more than flirted with this idea. I have also found that among sympathetic scholars of religion it is something of a point of honor to believe this. Nonetheless, for various reasons it is a concept I find thoroughly unconvincing, as only someone could who entitled a book on the subject *Up from Eden*.

The second way out of this impasse is to open the possibility that there are stages of structuralization higher than formal operational thinking. Ontogenetically, this would mean that an individual today can develop beyond exclusively rational forms of mentation to some sort of higher stage or stages of consciousness as yet unspecified. Phylogenetically, it means that evolution is still continuing and that human culture at large faces further and higher levels of (r)evolutionary structuralization.

But that idea reminds us immediately of Hegel,[45] who saw history as eventually transcending mental self-consciousness in the absolute knowledge of spirit as spirit. There are Aurobindo,[7] who maintained that evolution is driving toward supermind realization; Teilhard de Chardin,[91] who saw it culminating in omega point, or Christ consciousness at large; and the great Russian philosopher Berdyaev,[15] who concluded that evolution moves from subconsciousness to self-consciousness to superconsciousness (his words). Despite the excesses of some of these presentations, the point is that the general concept of evolution continuing beyond its present stage into some legitimately transrational structures is not a totally outrageous notion. Look at the course of evolution to date: from amoebas to humans! Now what if that ratio, amoeba-to-human, were applied to future evolution? That is, amoebas are to humans as humans are to—what? Is it ridiculous to suggest that the "what" might indeed be omega, *geist*, supermind, spirit? That subconscious is to self-conscious as self-conscious is to superconscious? That prepersonal gives way to personal, which gives way to transpersonal? That Brahman is not only the *ground* of evolution but the *goal* as well?

What is specifically needed, however, beyond these generalizations, is some sort of more precise specification of what the higher structure-stages of consciousness might be. For various reasons, I first looked to the psychological systems of Hinduism and Buddhism for possible answers; I later found these answers echoed in Sufism, Kabbalah, neo-

Confucianism, mystical Christianity, and other esoteric traditions. What struck me about these traditional psychologies is that, although they often lacked the detailed sophistication of modern Western psychologies, they were perfectly aware of the general features of the level-structures so intensively investigated in the West (i.e., physical, sensorimotor, emotional-sexual, lower mental, and logic-rational). Nonetheless, they universally claimed that these levels by no means exhausted the spectrum of consciousness—there were, beyond the physical, emotional, and mental levels, higher levels of structural organization and integration.

For instance, Vedanta Hinduism claims there are six major structure-levels of consciousness.[26] The first and lowest is called annamayakosha, literally the level made of physical food, or the physical body. The second is pranamayakosha, the level of emotional-sexuality (prana is an almost exact equivalent of libido). The third is manomayakosha, the level of mind. This level also includes, besides rationality, the "dream aspects" of mentation; dreams, says Shankara, are basically wish-fulfillments, composed of the person's "fantasy and desires." The fourth is vijnanamayakosha, higher mental or transrational or intuitive cognition, the beginning of actual spiritual insight. The fifth is anandamayakosha, the level of ecstatic illumination-insight. The highest state is *turiya,* or Brahman-Atman itself, although it is not so much one level among other levels but the ground, reality, or suchness of all levels (*tathata,* the Buddhists call it).

Anyway, I undertook an explicitly hermeneutic reading of the world's great traditional psychologies, attempting to analyze and interpret the general structural units of meaning presented in the various classic texts. I practiced Zen Buddhism under various teachers for ten years, so I know at least one tradition "from the inside," via empathetic participation.

The result of this hermeneutical and practical encounter with the traditional psychologies was presented in *The Atman Project,*[101] although in an extremely skeletal fashion and without methodological explanation. The conclusion was that it is indeed plausible that there are higher stages of structural organization and integration, and that these higher stages increasingly display what can only be called a spiritual or transcendental tone. These higher structure-stages I called, largely after Vedanta, the psychic, the subtle, the causal, and the ultimate levels. If we add these higher stages to figure 1, then we arrive at a tentative overall scheme of the developmental and structural spectrum of consciousness (see figure 2; Brahman—or Dharmakaya or Keter or Godhead—is said

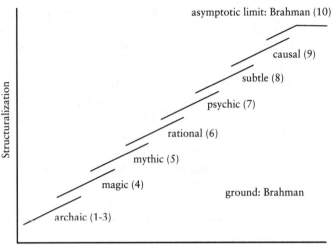

FIGURE 2

to be both the limit-at-infinity of growth, which I have listed as the asymptote, and the ever-present ground of all levels of growth, which can be represented by the paper itself, which I have labeled "ground").

We can also draw this as a circle and then more easily add the three large domains of development—subconscious (prepersonal), self-conscious (personal), and superconscious (transpersonal)—although their precise alignments with the specific structures are, of course, somewhat arbitrary. (See figure 3.)

Let me very briefly describe the higher or transpersonal levels, as disclosed in the various texts themselves. At the same time, I will correlate these levels with the basic types of *esoteric religious practice,* as suggested by such spiritual adepts as Aurobindo[7] and Free John,[22] and the Vajrayana tradition.[101]

The *psychic level** does not necessarily or even usually refer to paranormal events, although some texts say these can more readily or controllably occur here. More specifically, the psychic level can be best understood in reference to the level preceding it, that of formal opera-

---

* In this book I am treating the centauric and the psychic as one domain: as the great transition from personal to transpersonal. Technically, vision-logic is centauric (the "highest" of the personal realms), and vision is psychic (the "lowest" or beginning of the transpersonal realms), but they can, for convenience, be treated together as the transition into the spiritual domains.

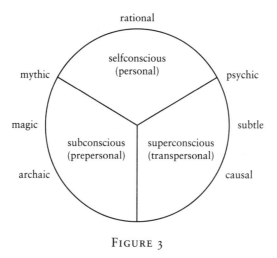

FIGURE 3

tional or propositional reasoning, whose form is "if a, then b." The psychic level simply works with or operates on the results of formal mentation. That is, where the formal mind establishes higher relationships ("if a, *then* b"), psychic cognition establishes *networks* of those relationships. The point is to place each proposition alongside numerous others, so as to be able to see, or "to vision," how the truth or falsity of any one proposition would affect the truth or falsity of the others. Such panoramic or *vision-logic* (the technical term I use to describe the cognitive operations of this level) apprehends a mass network of ideas, how they influence each other, what their relationships are. It is thus the beginning of truly higher-order synthesizing capacity, of making connections, relating truths, coordinating ideas, integrating concepts. It culminates in what Aurobindo called the "higher mind." It "can freely express itself in single ideas, but its most characteristic movement is a mass ideation, a system or totality of truth-seeing at a single view; the relations of idea with idea, of truth with truth, self-seen in the integral whole."

This is obviously a highly *integrative* structure. Although it might be thought of as the first and lowest of the transpersonal levels [psychic], it might also be described as the last and highest of the personal structures [centauric], beyond which lie more transcendental occasions. This highly integrated, highest personal structure is, in my opinion, generally correlated with Loevinger's integrated and autonomous stages, Maslow's self-actualization needs, Broughton's integrated stage, and so forth. (In Eastern systems, this is the sixth chakra, the beginning of manas and vijnanamayakosha, Tiferet, etc.)

Many orthodox psychologists have already suggested that there are probably one or more cognitive stages beyond formal operational. Bruner, for instance, believes that some adults may progress from being intelligent (formal operational) to being intelligent about intelligence (or operating on formal operations). The structure we are proposing here— vision-logic—seems to fit that bill exactly, with the added advantage that it meshes explicitly with various Eastern systems (as expressly stated by, for example, Aurobindo, as the above quote makes clear).

Owing to the intense panoramic awareness offered at this level—or rather, at its most mature and highly developed state*—the individual might begin to experience intense insight and even illumination, illumination that seems to go beyond thought into a type of vision, noetic, numinous, inspiring, often enstatic, occasionally ecstatic.[7,22] This can also result in a type of nature cosmic consciousness, or merging of self with the naturic universe (not to be confused with theistic or monistic mystical experiences, as we will see).[7] Those adepts mastering such states, via body manipulation and mental concentration, are generally known as *yogis*.

This does not mean that all who call themselves "yogis" actually attain this level. Nor does it mean that those who call themselves yogis never proceed higher than this level. It is just that the traditions that specifically describe themselves as *yogic* more often than not embody and express an understanding that most centrally reflects the psychic level, as clearly explained by Free John.[22] In the terms of chakra psychology, classic yogic discipline (hatha, kundalini, and ashtanga yoga) most centrally deals with those energies and insights leading from the first or root chakra, at the base of the spine, up through the sixth or ajna chakra, the "blue pearl," the "third eye," between and behind the brows. The ajna chakra is the embodiment of the psychic structure as here described. Beyond that point, consciousness leaves the psychic and enters the subtle.

The subtle level is said to be the seat of actual archetypes, of Platonic forms, of subtle sounds and audible illuminations *(nada, shabd)*, of transcendent insight and absorption.[22,85,86,105] Some traditions, such as Hinduism and Gnostic Christianity, claim that, according to direct phenomenological apprehension, this level is the home of personal deity-

---

* In other words, the difference between centauric vision-logic and psychic vision.

form (*ishtadeva,* demiurge, *yidam*), cognized in a stage known as *savikalpa samadhi* in Hinduism.[26,86,117] Overall, this is the level of the "illumined mind" (Aurobindo); the culmination of manas and vijna-mayakosha; a truly transrational structure (not prerational and not anti-rational); intuition in its highest and most sober sense (gnosis, jnana, prajna), not emotionalism or merely bodily felt meaning or vegetative-pranic-privatistic "hunch"; home of archangelic forms or ideas; bija-mantra, vasanas; beginning of seventh chakra (the *sahasrara*); and, of course, the start of Maslow's *self-transcendence needs.*

Those adepts who master these subtle realms of halos of truth and light, revelations of subtle sound, and direct soul-God-communion are generally known as *saints.* Again, this does not mean that all who call themselves saints have reached this level, nor that some authentic saints do not surpass this level. It means only that the disciplines, practices, and insights of the saintly traditions tend most centrally to reflect the subtle level of structural organization. In the terms of shabd chakra psychology, the subtle region begins at the sixth or ajna chakra, continues into the seventh or sahasrara, and then discloses several more levels of subtler and subtler hierarchic structures secreted within and beyond the sahasrara itself. Those adepts who master such subtle structures—nicely symbolized (both East and West) by halos of light at the crown of the head (sahasrara)—are generically referred to as saints. Beyond these saintly revelations, however, lies the causal/ultimate ground itself, or radical and transcendental Consciousness as Such.

The *causal level* is said to be the unmanifest source or transcendental ground of all the lesser structures, what Aurobindo called the "over-mind." It is realized in a stage of consciousness known variously as *nirvikalpa samadhi* (Hinduism), *nirodh* (Theravada Buddhism), *jnana samadhi* (Vedanta), the eighth of the ten ox-herding pictures (of Zen). This is the anandamayakosha (Vedanta), the *alayavijnana* (Mahayana), Keter, and so forth. Passing fully through the state of cessation or un-manifest absorption, consciousness is said finally to reawaken to its ab-solutely prior and eternal abode as spirit, radiant and all-pervading, one and many, only and all. This is classical, *sahaj samadhi,* the state-condi-tion of *turiya,* transcendental and unqualifiable consciousness as such, Aurobindo's "supermind," Zen's "One Mind," Brahman-Atman itself, Ein Sof, the Svabhavikakaya, and such. Throughout this book I will, for convenience, treat the causal and ultimate "levels" as one—spirit in the highest sense, not as a Big Person but as the "Ground of Being" (Tillich), "Eternal Substance" (Spinoza), "Geist" (Hegel), the ground *and* the goal of development-revolution itself.

The causal/ultimate level does not involve any particular experience but rather the dissolution or transcendence of the experiencer itself, the death of the watcher principle. That is, the subject-object duality is radically transcended, so that the soul no longer contemplates Divinity, it becomes Divinity, a release the Sufi calls the Supreme Identity. If the subtle is the home of God and God-communion, the causal/ultimate is the home of Godhead and Godhead Identity.[7,22,26,81,86,101,117]

At that stage, asymptotic at infinity, one becomes radically egoless, or free of the separate self sense, thus assuming an absolute identity with all manifestation, high or low, sacred or profane. And yet, in being one with everything, only and all, there is nothing other to this state, and so it appears perfectly, radically, paradoxically *ordinary*, as in the famous Zen saying, "How marvelous, how transcendental this! I draw water, I carry fuel." The adepts who realize this adaptation are generally known as *sages*.

As an example of the distinction between subtle saints and causal sages, we may take the Mosaic and Christic epiphanies.[105] The Mosaic revelation on Mount Sinai has all the standard features of a subtle level apprehension: a numinous Other that is Light, Fire, Insight, and Sound (shabd). Nowhere, however, does Moses claim to be one with or identical with that Being. In India, at roughly the same time, a similar level of religious insight was expressed in the Vedas. Christ, on the other hand, does claim that "I and the Father are one," a perfect Atmic or causal level apprehension. In India, also at about the same time, a similar understanding was being set down in the Upanishads, where we find such causal/ultimate and Christic-equivalent statements as "Thou art That," "This Atman is Brahman," "I am Brahman," and such, with the proviso that *anyone* can potentially attain this supreme identity, a tenet that was retained in Gnostic Christianity but lost/denied in exoteric-mythic Christianity, where Christ got "kicked upstairs," taking the supreme identity with him. Anyway, the difference between subtle saints and causal sages, or between the Mosaic-Vedic and Christic-Upanishadic revelations, is essentially the difference between savikalpa and nirvakalpa samadhi: in the former, one sees Being, in the latter, one becomes Being.

The point is that not only is there a variety of religious experience, there is a *hierarchy* of religious experience, with each successive stage—psychic, subtle, causal—being higher (by developmental, structural, and integrative standards) than its predecessor, and each correlative practice—yogic, saintly, and sagely—being likewise more ultimately revelatory.[105] This schema and its impact on the sociology of religion will be explored in chapters 6 and 7. For the moment, let us simply note that this scheme enters decisively into the debate started by Zaehner and still raging among scholars of religion.

Zaehner[134] began by clearly and correctly pointing out that "what goes by the name of mysticism, so far from being an identical expression of the selfsame Universal Spirit, falls into three distinct categories," which are panenhenic or nature mysticism (e.g., Rimbaud, Wordsworth), monistic mysticism (e.g., Vedanta, Zen), and theistic mysticism (e.g., Christianity). Zaehner then used this scheme in an attempt to give theistic mysticism a higher status than panenhenic and monistic mysticism. Ninian Smart,[134] on the other hand, wants to champion the nondualist schools of religion (Vedanta, Mahayana, etc.) as being, if not higher than, then at least not inferior to theistic mysticism, and so consequently attempts to defuse Zaehner's position by denying the distinction between theistic and monistic mysticism, although he does accept the clear distinction between them and panenhenic mysticism.

To my mind, both are partially right. There *is* a distinction between panenhenic, theistic, and monistic mystical experience; they correspond almost precisely to the levels of structural organization we have termed psychic, subtle, and causal. But we turn the structural tables on Zaehner and side with Smart: theistic religion is not higher than monistic; in fact, the opposite: saintly communion with spirit is transcended by sagely identity with spirit. Thus, for example, when Watts[94] argues that monistic mysticism includes theistic mysticism, but not vice versa, he intuitively invokes the principle of hierarchization that adjudicates degrees of comprehensive validity.

Such, then, is one (simplified) version of a nested hierarchy of structural organization, one that includes prepersonal or subconscious components, personal or self-conscious components, and transpersonal or superconscious components. Whether or not that scheme is valid—indeed, the overall methodology of verifying (or rejecting) such schemes—will be explicitly dealt with in chapter 9. In the meantime, we may *hypothetically* or provisionally accept it as valid.* We will simply *assume* it is more or less the case and see if acting on this assumption helps clarify the psychology and sociology of religion. In the next two chapters, we will fill in a few more details of this overall model or hypothesis. Then, in chapter 5, we will indeed begin acting on it.

---

* [See *Integral Psychology* for extensive cross-cultural comparisons of this spectrum of consciousness.]

3

The Compound Individual
as a Link between Psychology
and Sociology

STRUCTURES ARE STRUCTURES OF
RELATIONAL EXCHANGE

WHAT MAKES THE ABOVE SCHEME—the ten or so levels of structural organization—not merely of relevance to sociology but somehow fused with sociology is the nature of each level itself. Namely, as *Up from Eden* tried to demonstrate, each level is a *process of exchange* with *corresponding* levels of structural organization in the world process at large, and that makes its psychology always also social psychology, as this chapter will now suggest.

For convenience's sake, I will reduce the number of levels of structural organization to five and use the names most familiar to Westerners: matter (1), body (2–3), mind (4–6), soul (7–8), and spirit (9–10). Now, since each of these levels of structural organization *transcends but includes* its predecessors, each structure of development enfolds, envelops, comprehends, or *compounds* the previous structures, much as the neocortex envelops the mammalian limbic system, which in turn envelops the reptilian stem.[100] Again, a nested hierarchy, a development that is envelopment.

For this reason, and in an explicit attempt to connect developmental psychology and evolution theory with the philosophical groundwork of Whitehead[97] and Hartshorne,[44] we say that the human being is a *compound individual*—compounded of all the past levels of development and capped by the present level itself. Potentially, then, the human being is *compounded* of matter, prana, mind, soul, and spirit. The material body is exercised in labor with the physical-natural environment; the pranic (emotional) body is exercised in breath, sex, and feeling with other pranic bodies; the mind is exercised in linguistic communication with other minds; the soul, in psychic and subtle relationships; the spirit, in absolute relation to and as Godhead (or God-communion and God-identity). That is, *each level of the compound human individual is exercised in a complex system of ideally unobstructed relationships with the corresponding levels of structural organization in the world process at large.*[105]

Furthermore, humanity actually and literally reproduces itself on each level by an appropriate *exchange* of the elements of that level (with corresponding levels in the world at large). Humanity reproduces itself physically through the exchange of food secured by labor from the natural environment. It reproduces itself bodily (or biologically) via exchange of breath and sex. It reproduces itself mentally via education and communicative exchange. It reproduces itself spiritually (soul and spirit) via living exchange-transmission from adept to disciple.[105]

It thus appears that each level is intrinsically part of a sliding chain of relational exchanges and therefore *is itself* most fundamentally a *society* of exchanges, or social relationship. Even the material body, the very lowest level, is a *process* of food intake, assimilation, and release, and thus is always bound not to but as the community of its exchange partners. Sexual reproduction is obviously relational exchange. As for the mental level, Lévi-Strauss (among many others) has clearly established that "in mathematics, in logic, or in life, a symbol must be exchanged with another person; in the act of exchange the symbol creates and maintains a relationship. Thus, the word *symbol* refers us back to the original Greek meaning: pact, bond, covenant, intercourse, or link."[107] And spiritual levels are not only exchanges with divinity, or communion-identity, but with divinity embodied as the spiritual master *and* the community of contemplative partners. Each level is a society of relationships or exchange occasions, with the human *compound* individual being an integral of those societies, hopelessly interlocked with other humans in societies of *those.*[105]

The notion of relational exchange is sometimes expressed (redundantly) in the concept of "drives" or "needs." Since each level in the human being *is* a process of relational exchange with a corresponding environment, the human being has drives that express the need for those various environments: physical needs (food, water, air, shelter), emotional needs (feeling, touch-contact, sex), mental-egoic needs (interpersonal communication, reflexive self-esteem, meaning), spiritual needs (God-communion, depth), and so on. It is as if there were levels of "food" or "mana"—physical food, emotional food, mental food, spiritual food. Growth and development is simply the process of adapting to, and learning to digest, subtler and subtler levels of food, with each stage of growth marked by a phase-specific adaptation to a particular type of food. (We will return to the concept of phase-specific mana in the next chapter.)

The point is simply that, because each structure-level *is* a process of relational exchange (or food-needs), it is *necessarily* wedded to the objects that "satisfy" those needs. "Structure," "need," and "object-relations" are simply three aspects of the single exchange process that is each level. Take away the need-objects or food of the structure, and one takes away the structure itself. Take away gross food, and the physical body begins to wither; take away vital food, feeling or warmth, and the emotional body begins to wither; take away "food for thought," intersubjective communication or symbolic exchange, and the mind begins to wither; take away transcendental food, spiritual relationship or grace-faith, and the soul begins to wither. In short, the notion of need or drive expresses nothing but the necessity for a structure to engage its corresponding object-relations or perish.

THE DISTORTION OF RELATIONAL EXCHANGE

The developmental nature of these levels of structural organization and relational exchange (or food-needs) should be emphasized, however, because all of these levels are not *manifest* in individual humans from birth. Rather, the human individual apparently begins its growth and development by adjusting to the physical world (and its food), then to the emotional world (and its food), then the verbal-mental, then the transcendental, and so on (until growth stops in its own case). While these developments often parallel or overlap one another, nonetheless each level is built upon, and rests upon, the foundation afforded by its immediately junior level. However, and in my opinion this cannot be overemphasized, while the higher level "rests on" the lower, the higher is not caused by or constituted by the lower. The higher is in part *emergent,* discontinuous, milestone, revolutionary. The higher emerges *by way of* the lower; it comes *through* the lower, so to speak, but not *from* it, much as a baby chick comes through its eggshell but is not made of eggshells. For example, mind comes *through* libido, not *from* it.[105]

As the higher begins to emerge, it has to pass through the lower for the simple reason that the lower is *already* there, it already exists. As the higher appears on the scene, the scene *is* the lower or immediately junior dimension itself, and the higher is thus initially fused and confused with that lower—it is initially *undifferentiated* from it. Growth of the higher level is in part the process of vertical transcendence or *differentiation* from (and then integration of) the lower level through which it passed on its own emergence.[101]

Thus, for example, prior to age $1\frac{1}{2}$ or so, the infant cannot clearly differentiate the bodyself from the physical environment; it lives in a state of protoplasmic indissociation (Piaget: "the self is here material, so to speak")[70]; bodyself and material world are largely undifferentiated. Between the ages of $1\frac{1}{2}$ to 3 or so, the infant learns to differentiate the bodyself from the objective physical world, thus allowing the body to transcend that primitive-material fusion state.[50] As the symbolic mind begins to emerge (around 24 months or so), it is then initially undifferentiated from the body itself—mind and body are fused and confused (thinking is physiognomic, as Werner put it, or contaminated with sensorimotor categories, according to Piaget).[95,70] It is not until around age 7 or so that mind and body are first differentiated, and not until age 11–15 that they are clearly differentiated and mind finally transcends (but subsumes) the body itself.[57,70] Likewise, when (and if) the soul eventually emerges, it is initially fused and confused with the mind (it is clothed in mental forms and thoughts, not yet its own intrinsic visions and illuminations), and so on. The point is that in each case the higher emerges through, or by way of, the lower, only transcending the lower when it finally differentiates from it. This process of separation-individuation, or transcendence-and-integration, marks each major stage of growth or emergence.[101] But we repeat: although the higher comes through the lower, it does not come *from* the lower, its essence being in part emergent.

Nonetheless, this emergence *through* the lower can have fateful consequences, because a distorted lower can *incline* the higher to subsequently reproduce the distortion on its own domain, much as a tough or brittle eggshell can damage the chick in its emergence. Perhaps a better metaphor here is a skyscraper: because the higher both comes through and then rests upon the foundation of the lower, a "tilt" in the first floor tends to cause a similar tilt in the second, and so on. Physical trauma can lead to emotional disturbances; emotional disturbances can generate mental instabilities, and so on.

But this is not an absolute causality; not only is the lower distortion only partially passed on, but *the higher level, by virtue of its emergent freedom, can often redress the imbalance.* We say, then, that a distortion in the lower *predisposes* (but does not cause) the higher to reproduce similar if dampened distortions in its own domain.

On the other side of the fence, the higher, because it does partially transcend the lower, can *repress* the lower. For example, sex cannot easily repress sex, but mind can repress sex, simply because mind is higher in structural organization than sex and can thus "come down on" sex.

Repression, as I use the term, is fundamentally an *internal* affair; it is instigated by the separate self in order to defend its own precarious sense of existence in the face of prior and always apprehended mortality. Repression is not caused by others or instigated by others, and it will occur, to various degrees, in even the most idyllic surroundings, simply because no setting is free of the skull that, as James said, will soon grin in at the banquet. Any aspect of the self-system—sensation, perception, emotion, cognition—that becomes too threatening, too laden with death-guilt, too charged with taboo, will be split from the system, outlawed, banished. Such repression does not actually destroy the "shadow," however, but merely sends it underground, where it registers its existence by sending up cryptic symbols (the hidden text) and disturbing symptoms.[101,105]

Although one individual cannot directly repress another, one individual can *oppress* another. This oppression has several consequences, two of which are (1) the oppression can disrupt and distort the exchange processes and capacities of any and all levels of the compound individual (as Marx found out for *material* exchange, Freud for *emotional-sexual* exchange, Socrates for *mental* communicative exchange, and Christ for *spiritual* exchange); and (2) the separate self, as it endures in (and attempts to adapt and adjust to) the atmosphere of such oppression, can and will *internalize* the originally external oppression, and *internalized oppression* then leads to *surplus repression,* repression over and above that which the self would induce on its own.[105]

Here are our generalizations so far: (1) the higher comes *through* the lower but not *from* the lower; (2) a distorted lower *inclines* the higher to reproduce similar distortions in its own sphere but (3) does not absolutely *cause* the higher to reproduce the distortions (the higher can to some degree dampen, reverse, amend, compensate, etc.); (4) the individual can defensively *repress* or internally distort, to one degree or another, any or all of his own levels of exchange (physical, emotional, mental, spiritual); (5) an external (powerful) other can *oppress* and distort an individual's levels of exchange; and (6) internalized oppression is surplus repression.

The Backbone of a Comprehensive Critical Theory in Sociology

I have elsewhere suggested how these generalizations can help us to reconstruct the essentials of such theorists as Marx and Freud without their reductionistic tendencies.[105] For, as we look at the levels of structural organization and relational exchange of the compound individual, it becomes obvious that many theorists have taken *one* level and tried to make it paradigmatic. If they take a higher level, as idealists do, they tend to elevate the lower levels to an exalted status they simply do not possess, or they tend to ignore the lower levels altogether. Reading history according to Hegel, for instance, one always gets the impression that the material world might at any moment evaporate. This apparently annoyed Marx so much that he took the opposite but perfectly standard reductionistic approach: take a lower level, call it "the only really real" level, then reduce all higher levels to it, or at least explain all higher levels in terms of the lower. I need not tell you that Marx made the material level and its exchanges paradigmatic for *all* forms of existence. Freud did *exactly* the same thing for the next level up; emotional-sexual energies are *the* reality, and all else—culture, ego, mind, religion—is just a sneaky twisting of libido. At the next level up, we often find theorists who admirably refuse to reduce mental consciousness to sexual offsprings or material modes of production and, instead, accord mind its own rightful and higher place in development, but they tend to deny validity to realms higher than mind, realms that they then subject to standard reductionism—such "spiritual realities" are, at best, merely functional symbols without *real* referents. Communication becomes paradigmatic for such theorists (e.g., Habermas), and direct spiritual awareness is accorded something of a derivative status at best.

But you can see where such theorists *have* made absolutely crucial—if absolutely partial—contributions. Marx, for instance, compellingly demonstrated that when the material-economic exchange process is oppressed and distorted, then upon that distorted base tends to emerge alienated thoughts and feelings, or "false consciousness," and that the higher cultural productions of art, philosophy, and religion are thereby pressed as ideology into mere servants of oppression, each becoming, in its own way, an "opiate of the masses." Similarly, Freud demonstrated that emotional-sexual distortions tilted mental consciousness toward symptomatic sclerosis, blocked the free flow of mental ideas, and generally set up another type of false consciousness in the form of a façade or pseudo-self alienated from aspects of its own being (because it is alienated from aspects of relational exchanges *with others,* hence the modern emphasis on object-relations theory).

Now we want to take all of those essentials with us, but without their reductionism. For both Marx and Freud went from saying, "A distorted lower predisposes the higher to similar distortions" (correct), to saying, "The distortions in the higher stem almost entirely from the distortions in the lower" (incorrect; they stem partially from them, but they can also be distorted for reasons purely their own), to saying, "The higher itself must therefore come from a distortion or frustration of the lower" (even more incorrect; that amounts to making the dynamics of repression/oppression paradigmatic for the whole of development), to saying, "If there were no frustration of the lower, there would be *no* higher" (patently absurd, but the reductionism is here completed). Hence the orthodox Marxist position that when material exchanges are finally communalized, there will be *no need for* philosophy, art, religion, and so forth; and the precisely correlative Freudian notion that without frustration of instinctual urges, the mind would never emerge and develop. Thus we utilize the valid insights of such theorists with the second generalization; we counteract their reductionism with the first and third generalizations.

My point is that a comprehensive, unified, critical sociological theory might best be constructed around a detailed, multidisciplinary analysis of the developmental-logic and hierarchic levels of relational (psychosocial) exchanges that constitute the human compound individual. The theory would be *critical* in two important ways: (1) adjudicative of each *higher* level of structural organization and critical of the comparative partiality of each lower level, and (2) critical of the *distortions* in exchange when and if they occur on any particular level. The latter is a criticism *within* a level and demands as its corrective a self-reflection on the historical formations that led to the distortion in the particular realm, economic, emotional, communicative, or spiritual. The former is a criticism *between* levels and demands as its corrective a *growth* to higher levels. The one is a horizontal emancipation, the other, a vertical emancipation. Neither can be dispensed with—growth to a higher level does not ensure the healthy normalization of a lower level, and healing a lower level does not in and of itself produce a higher level. (We will return to this topic in chapter 8.)

At a minimum, then, our levels of analysis would include (1) the physical level of material exchange, whose paradigm is food consumption and food extraction from the natural environment, whose sphere is that of manual (technic) labor, and whose archetypal analyst is Marx; (2) the emotional level of pranic (vital) exchange, whose paradigm is breath and sex, whose sphere is that of emotional intercourse, from feeling to sex to power, and whose archetypal analyst is Freud; (3) the mental level of symbolic exchange, whose paradigm is discourse (language), whose sphere is that of communication, and whose archetypal analyst is Socrates; (4) the psychic level of intuitive exchange, whose paradigm is siddhi (or psychic insight and vision in general), whose sphere is yogic kundalini, and whose archetypal analyst is Patanjali; (5) the subtle level of God-Light exchange, whose paradigm is shabd-revelation and subtle illumination (savikalpa samadhi), whose sphere is saintly "heaven" (Brahma-Loka, the higher structural potentials of one's own compound individuality), and whose archetypal analyst is Moses/Saint Paul/Kirpal Singh; and (6) the causal level of infinite exchange, whose paradigm is radical absorption in and as the Uncreate (nirvikalpa/sahaj samadhi), whose sphere is sagely Godhead, and whose archetypal analyst is Buddha/Krishna/Christ.[105]

4

Translation, Transformation, Transcription

GENERAL DEFINITIONS

B EFORE WE FINALLY APPLY this general theory to such specifics as
the sociology of religion, new religions, cults, and such, we need a
few technical definitions. If we simplistically think of the various levels
of structural organization as so many floors in a tall building (in this
case, ten stories, with tenth being Brahman as highest level and asymptotic limit of growth, and the building itself being Brahman as the
ground of all levels of growth), then (1) each floor itself is a *deep structure,* while (2) the variable components on each floor—its actual furniture, so to speak—are *surface structures;* (3) the movement of surface
structures we call *translation;* (4) the movement of deep structures we
call *transformation;* and (5) the relation between a deep structure and its
surface structures we call *transcription.* Translation is moving furniture
around on one floor; transformation is moving to a different floor; transcription is the relation of the furniture to each floor.

 As a more accurate example, take a game such as checkers or chess.
The surface structures are the various pieces and the various moves they
make in a given game. The deep structure is the *rules* of the game, the
patterns that define the *internal relations* of the various pieces to each
other. The rules holistically unite each piece to each other via patterned
relations. The deep structure *defines the game*—you can alter the surface

structures, make the pieces out of clay, plastic, or wood, and you still have the same basic game. You can even use rocks; all you have to do is transcribe the pieces according to the basic rules, that is, show how each piece fits into the rules of the deep structure. That relation of deep to surface structures is *transcription*. Finally, actually moving the pieces around on the board, or executing a play, is *translation*.

Now if we change the deep structure, we change the basic rules of the game, and then obviously it is no longer the same game. We have *transformed* it into something else—perhaps another good game, perhaps a mess. Sometimes people will take checkers pieces and a checkerboard (if they do not want to buy a chess set) and transform them into chess by first changing the rules, or transforming the deep structure to that of chess; then transcribing the checkers according to their functions in chess, which means marking them as a rook, king, pawn, and so forth; and then finally translating these new surface structures according to the deep rules of chess.

Notice, even in this simple example, that the deep structures do not themselves change during the course of a game, nor are they influenced by the particular moves of a particular game. They are "a-historical." The surface structures do change, however, for each sequence of moves is different from game to game. What determines the particular course of moves is the sum of previous moves in the game so far. That is, the next move I make in a particular game will occur *within* the rules of the deep structure, but it is determined specifically by all the preceding moves (plus my present judgment about those previous moves). Those surface structures, in other words, are *historically conditioned*—not totally caused, but definitely molded to some degree, by past surface structures.

That is a small example of an overall postulate that refers to the basic levels of structural organization themselves: insofar as they have emerged, the deep structures of consciousness (e.g., as presented in figure 2) are relatively a-historical, collective, invariant, and cross-cultural, whereas their surface structures are everywhere variable, historically conditioned, and culturally molded.[105] Thus, for example, the deep structure of the formal operational mind is, as far as we know, identical wherever it emerges, but the actual surface forms of that mind—its particular belief systems, ideologies, languages, customs, and so forth—are everywhere different, molded largely by the culture in which that mind itself develops.[70] This postulate (or rather, experimental conclusion) is similar to Chomsky's universal-grammar/specific-cultural-semantics,[24] except that it is not confined to the mental/linguistic levels but refers to all levels of basic structural organization (e.g., the deep structure of the physical body is everywhere identical—208 bones, 2 kidneys, 4 limbs, 1 heart, etc.—but the surface activities of that body—the acceptable forms of play, work, sports, etc.—differ from culture to culture; and so on with emotional, subtle, causal, and other levels of structural organization). The idea itself took its initial impetus from Jung's work on archetypes as "forms devoid of content"[53] (although see Wilber[102]), but was bolstered by the cross-cultural investigations related to the work of Piaget, Kohlberg, Werner, and others. That this conclusion also and expressly applies to the deep and surface structures of the three stages of religious-mystical experience (psychic, subtle, causal) should especially be noted, for we will be drawing on this point in chapter 7.

THE FUNCTION OF TRANSLATION: MANA AND TABOO

Development or growth, then, seems to occur in two primary dimensions: horizontal-evolutionary-historical and vertical-revolutionary-transcendental, or, in short, translative and transformative. Horizontal or translative growth is a process of transcribing, filling in, or "fleshing out" the surface structures of a given level; that is, assuming responsibility for the relational exchange of surface structures that constitutes the very lifeline or "food" of that level, a process that must occur if that level and the society of its reciprocal exchange partners are to reproduce themselves both moment to moment (or individually) and generation to generation (or collectively). Transformation, on the other hand, is a vertical shift, a revolutionary reorganization of past elements and emergence of new ones. It is synonymous with *transcendence,* although notice that transcendence is then not confined to the upper levels of consciousness (although it occurs there royally), but rather refers to the fact that *each* successive level transcends or goes beyond its predecessor(s): myth transcends magic, reason transcends myth, soul transcends reason, spirit transcends soul.[101]

Translation apparently has one major function: to integrate, stabilize, and equilibrate its given level; transformation apparently has one major function: to go beyond its given level. This dialectic of tensions seems to constitute much of the dynamic of development.[95,102] In this section, we key on its translative dimension.

Translation's major function—to integrate, stabilize, and equilibrate its given level—seems to have two basic facets, which we call *mana* and *taboo*.[105] Mana refers to the "food" of each level: for example, physical food, emotional food (love, belongingness), mental food (symbol, truth), spiritual food (illumination, insight). Translation is involved in securing the mana-food of its particular level via, of course, the processes of relational exchange (reception, assimilation, and release), for mana-food is exactly what *is* exchanged in those processes. Further, it seems that mana-translation, by virtue of this *necessary* relationship in and as a society of exchange partners, establishes and constitutes, in all of its phase-specific forms, the "glue" that binds the particular society in which the exchanges occur. With that in mind, and on any given level, we define "good mana" as that which is integrative, healthy, legitimate, and intrinsically binding, both within the boundaries of the particular individual and between the boundaries of individuals in the exchange process at large. "Bad mana," conversely, is less integrative or even disintegrative for the particular level.

We also suggest that, besides good and bad mana within a level, there are higher and lower forms of mana between levels. That is, each progressively higher level of structural organization seems to have access to a progressively higher mana, or higher truth-food. This does not, however, deny the relative and *phase-specific validity* of the lower truths. Nor does it, in and by itself, guarantee integrative stability for the higher level, since the bad mana of a higher level is often less integrative than the good mana of a lower one. But the potential for higher truth and integration is most definitely present, and so on balance we say that, for example, science is more truthful than myth just as saintly illumination is truer than science, but all serve their necessary and phase-specific functions and deliver themselves of appropriate-enough truths. Vertical growth is a series of phase-specific adaptations to increasingly higher levels of food, mana, truth, while horizontal growth is a process of learning to digest (intake, assimilation, release) that food on its own level.

For the taboo facet of translation, I have explicitly tied my arguments into those of Rank,[74] Becker,[10] and Brown,[19] although again I have tried to avoid what I feel are reductionistic elements in their theories. Their position is basically existential; it deals with the impact of death-apprehension on the individual psyche and the resultant attempts to deal with, or deny, the terror of mortality.

For *death,* they maintain, is *the* fundamental taboo, the fundamental terror, and to the extent the separate self awakens to its own existence, then to that extent terror-angst is *inherent* in the self. ("The essential, basic arch-anxiety is innate to all isolated, individual forms of human existence. In the basic anxiety human existence is afraid *of* as well as anxious *about* its 'being-in-the-world.' ") Thus, there is simply but absolutely no way to avoid that terror except by repression or some other defensive or compensatory mechanism. Angst is not something the self suffers; it is something the self *is*.

Now the traditional psychologies—Hinduism and Buddhism, for example—agree perfectly and explicitly with that assessment (Buddha is regarded by many scholars, myself included, as having given *the* existential statement and analysis of the human predicament: anicca, anatta, dukkha—fleeting, selfless, pain). Wherever there is self, there is trembling; wherever there is other, there is fear. However—and this is where the traditions transcend mere existentialism—these psychologies maintain that one can go beyond fear and trembling by going beyond self and other; that is, by transcending subject and object in satori, moksha, the supreme identity.

But those traditions also maintain that the great liberation finally takes place only at the sagely level of causal/ultimate adaptation.[22,28,105] All lesser stages, no matter how occasionally ecstatic or visionary, are still beset with the primal mood of ego, which is sickness unto death. Even the saint, according to the sages, has yet to finally surrender his or her soul, or separate-self sense, and this prevents the saint from attaining absolute identity with and as Godhead.[22] Since the separate-self sense forms very early in development—a primitive series of ego nuclei arise within months of birth[17]—and since it does not finally uncoil until the sagely level of structural adaptation, it follows that all levels of development, short of the great liberation, are marked by the separate self. And the separate self *is* a contraction of angst; specifically, a fear of its own death or nonbeing.

It was Otto Rank[73,74] who supplied the necessary psychodynamic characteristic of this state of affairs. The separate self, he said, faced with the fundamental taboo that is mortality, is forced, in order to attain a modicum of stability (translative equilibrium), to close its eyes to its own possible nonbeing. Put simply, it represses death ("Consciousness of death is the primary repression, not sexuality," as Becker[10] put it). One of the results of doing this, or one of the actual ways of doing this, said Rank, is by creating a series of *immortality symbols,* which, in their *promise* to transcend death, assuage the paralyzing cold that would otherwise freeze the self's operations.

If this is so, then translation deals not only with mana but with taboo, the basic taboo that is death, but a taboo that takes different and phase-specific forms on each level. From this angle, psycho-cultural productions could be seen (in part) to be *codified systems of death-denial* (I say "in part" because in my opinion that is half the truth; the other half is mana accumulation). It was Rank's genius to see that not only magic and myth but *rational* productions and purely logical beliefs were likewise immortality projects. They were productions that, in aspiring to some degree of truth, aspired to some degree of durability, and in aspiring to durability claimed hoped-for immortality ("My ideas will live on. . . ."). From that angle, culture—even rational culture—is what a separate self does with death: the self that is doomed only to die, and knows it, and spends its entire life (consciously or unconsciously) trying to deny it, both by manipulating its own subjective life and by erecting "permanent" and "timeless" cultural objects and conceptual principles as outward and visible signs of an inward and hoped-for immortality.

I will not repeat the entire argument of Rank, Becker, or Brown or my reformulation of its essentials. Take, instead, a simple summary by Becker: "Man from the very beginning could not live with the prospect of death. . . . Man erected cultural symbols which do not age or decay to quiet his fear of his ultimate end. This way of looking at the doings of man gives a direct key to the unlocking of history. We can see that what people want in any epoch is a way of transcending their physical fate, they want to guarantee some kind of indefinite duration, and culture provides them with the necessary immortality symbols or ideologies; societies can be seen as structures of immortality power."

In *Up from Eden,* I tried to show some of the phase-specific forms of such death-denial. It can be the immortality promised by magic ritual: "Where there is magic, there is no death,"[23] as Campbell summarized paleolithic religion. It can be the immortality promised by myth: "To be a favorite of the gods, to be an immortal," as Becker[11] would summarize classic mythic religion. It can be the immortality promised by reason: "The god of his own thought," said L. L. Whyte,[98] "which as recompense promises immortality." There even seems to be a very subtle form of immortality project in the soul realms: the last remnant of the separate self intuits timeless Being and then mistakes that timelessness for an *everlasting duration* or *permanent* self sense ("your immortal soul," which is no such thing; the Mahayana texts are always warning practitioners not to mistake the causal-alaya for a permanent soul).[88] The point is that, until there is final liberation—if such, indeed, exists—there remains some form of immortality project. Those projects become less and less compensatory at each higher level of structural organization, but they are never fully uprooted until the separate-self sense is itself uprooted. Prior to that time, life remains a battle of mana versus taboo.

In summary, the function of translation is to integrate, stabilize, and equilibrate its present level by securing mana and avoiding taboo in the process of relational exchange. This function obviously takes on different forms on different levels, but the function itself is present on all levels (functional invariant, Piaget calls it). Along with the basic deep structures, and the transformative functional invariant, this capacity seems to be part of the *native apparatus* of the self-system (cf. Hartmann's "inborn apparatus").[42]

TRANSFORMATION: DEATH AND REBIRTH ON EACH LEVEL

As we now turn to transformative or vertical development, it is a little more obvious what is involved: in order for an individual to transform to the next higher level, he or she has, in effect, to accept the *death* of the present level of adaptation, that is, to cease an *exclusive* identity with that level. Thus, for example, to progress to operational myth, the child has to give up or die to an exclusive allegiance to magical wishes; to progress to rational science, the adolescent has to give up an exclusive attachment to mythic outcomes; to progress to yogic adaptation, the adult has to surrender and release isolated-linear rationality into a larger intuitive vision, and so on.[101]

In each case, it is only when the self is *strong enough to die to that level* that it can *transcend* that level, that is, transform to the next higher level of phase-specific truth, food, mana. As the self identifies with the new level and begins to adapt to its food-mana, it *then* faces the fear of dying on and to *that* level, and its translative processes swing into gear to screen out the new version of always mortality that otherwise would freeze still the movement of self. The *new* self adapts to *new* truth-mana, faces *new* other, therefore suffers new death-seizure, therefore instigates new defense measures, and therefore, among other things, erects new immortality projects.[105]

Development, in this sense, is a series of progressively shedding immortality projects by progressively shedding the layers of self these projects were designed to protect, thereby simultaneously rising to new levels of phase-specific food, truth, mana. *Each* transformation is a process of death and rebirth: death to the old level, and transformation to and rebirth on the newly emergent level. And, according to the sages, when all layers of self have been transcended—when all deaths have been died—the result is only God in final Truth, and a new Destiny beyond destiny is resurrected from the stream of consciousness.

5

Some Usages of the Word "Religion"

O NE OF THE GREAT DIFFICULTIES in discussing religion—its sociology, its possible universality, its "civil" dimensions—is that it is
not an "it." In my opinion, "it" has at least a dozen different, major,
largely exclusive meanings, and unfortunately these are not always, not
even usually, distinguished in the literature. Let me point out some of
the ways we can (and do) use the word "religion," and what I believe is
actually behind each usage. My point will be that each of these usages is
legitimate enough—we are free to define religion any way we wish—but
we *must specify that meaning.* For what we will find is that many scholars have several implicit but often very different definitions in mind, and
they slip between these usages in a way that generates pseudo-conclu-
sions. I will number these religious definitions and subsequently refer to
them as rd-1, rd-2, and so on.

   1. *Religion as nonrational engagement.* This has both positive and
negative connotations. To theologians, it means that religion deals with
valid but nonrational aspects of existence, such as faith, grace, transcendence, satori, and such. To positivists, it means religion is nonvalid
knowledge; it might be "meaningful" to humans in an emotional way,
but it is not real cognition.

   This usage is often reflected in common sense. Most people would
intuitively say that magic-voodoo is a type of religion, however primitive, and that mythic gods and goddesses are definitely religious, although maybe not very "serious." They would also say that what yogis,
saints, and sages do is certainly religious. But science-rationality? *That*

is not religious. This overall usage says that religion is not so much something done on all levels but rather on particular levels, and specifically, those that are not rational-scientific per se. If you are pro-religion, then this definition implies that religion is something you can grow into; if con, something you hope to outgrow. In either case, it is nonrational; it belongs to or at least originates in a dimension that is other to reason.

2. *Religion as extremely meaningful or integrative engagement.* This usage says religion is not something that occurs on specific nonrational dimensions or levels but is a particular functional activity on any given level, an activity of seeking meaning, integration, etc. In my opinion, this usage actually reflects each level's search for mana—the search for meaning, truth, integrity, stability, and subject-object relationship (exchange). Since mana-translation, as we have seen, must occur on each level of structural organization, then whether that level appears "religious" or "secular" does not matter; it is religious, or mana-searching, by this definition.

This usage is also reflected in common sense. Thus, even the typical individual who initially says that myths, saints, sages, and such are religious but science is *not,* will usually understand exactly what you mean if you say, "Science was Einstein's religion." *Star Trek* fans say, "Logic is Spock's religion." Here, even purely rational endeavors are said to be religious, because they are, like all levels, in search of their phase-specific mana, and this mana-search—on *whatever* level, high or low, sacred or secular—is natively understood as religion.

Notice that, although both rd-1 and rd-2 are acceptable usages, they are nonetheless quite different, almost contradictory, and unless we specify which we mean, certain paradoxes and spurious conclusions will result. For instance, rd-1 denies secular religion, rd-2 demands it; rd-1 denies science is religion, rd-2 says it is (or can be). Both are acceptable, as long as we understand that behind the one word "religion" there are different functions. Oftentimes common sense will use both of these meanings without specifying them, thus producing a pseudo-paradox. The person might say, "Mr. Jones doesn't go to church; he doesn't believe in religion—money is his religion."

3. *Religion as an immortality project.* This is using the technical term we earlier introduced, but the actual term itself need not be invoked. The idea is simply that religion is fundamentally a wishful, defensive, compensatory belief, created in order to assuage insecurity/anxiety. This meaning is often applied to theology, but it is also used for rational and

secular endeavors, as when Becker says that Marxism is Soviet religion, meaning not just mana-search (rd-2) but death-denial. This can occur, as we have seen, on any level, and simply reflects that level's inherent taboo avoidance. In this particular function, science does *for* the rational ego exactly what *myth* does for the childish ego and *magic* does for the infantile ego—helps to veil the apprehension of ultimate and inescapable mortality by providing a belief system to "hang on to." This seems especially true of "scienticians," that is, scientists whose rd-2 religion (mana religion) happens to be science itself. I have found that, when push comes to shove, they will guard their exclusively Rational World View with a quivering passion every bit as charged with hoped-for immortality as that of a shrieking fundamentalist preacher. The point is simply that each level (short of the ultimate) tends to erect some sort of immortality project as part of its necessary defense structures, and this usage of religion simply keys on this particular function (although, typically, most of those who use this definition deny that there is any other).

4. *Religion as evolutionary growth.* This is a sophisticated concept maintaining that all evolution and history is a process of increasing self-realization, or the overcoming of alienation via the return *of* spirit *to* spirit *as* spirit. Hegel, for instance, or Aurobindo. In this sense, religion is actually a term for the transformative drive in general. The religious impulse here means, not searching for meaning, integration, mana or value *on* a given level (which is rd-2), but dying to that level altogether so as to find increasingly *higher* structures of mana-truth, eventuating in God-Realized Adaptation itself.

5. *Religion as fixation/regression.* We already discussed this usage; the only thing we need say here is that this meaning differs from rd-1 only in being more specific and always derogatory. Religion is not nonrational, it is prerational, and that exhausts the alternatives. This is standard primitivization theory: religion is childish illusion, magic, myth.

6. *Exoteric religion.* This generally refers to the lower, outward, and/or preparatory aspects of any religion that has higher, inward, and/or advanced aspects of teaching and practice. It is usually a form of *belief* system used to invoke or support *faith,* both being preparatory to esoteric *experience* and *adaptation* (see chapter 6 for those definitions). If a religion lacks an esoteric dimension altogether, then that religion on the whole is referred to as exoteric (the point of comparison being the esoteric dimensions of other religions).

7. *Esoteric religion.* This refers to the higher, inward, and/or advanced aspects of religious practise, with the proviso that such practices culminate in, or at least have as goal, mystical experience.

(For the next two definitions, we need a preliminary explanation. Once an author defines religion, he or she has automatically established some sort of criteria for "more valid" or "less valid" religion, simply because once the function of religion is actually specified, there are always better and worse cases. Now the nature of this "better or worse" depends upon the prior, basic definition the author gives to religion. If rd-1 is used—religion as a nonrational dimension or realm, and in this case it means higher realm—then valid religion, or more valid religion, comes implicitly or explicitly to mean actually contacting those authentic, higher realms or levels. On the other hand, if rd-2 is used—religion as search for mana on *any* level—then valid or more valid religion does not mean experiencing a particular level but finding legitimate mana on one's present level. These are obviously two entirely different meanings of "valid," and it presents a chronic semantic difficulty rarely acknowledged in the literature. I therefore have no choice but to use two different words—"authentic" and "legitimate"—to specify these two meanings of valid.)

8. *Legitimate religion.* This is religion that primarily *validates translation;* usually by providing "good mana" and helping avoid taboo, that is, providing units of meaning on the one hand and immortality symbols on the other. If an author (implicitly or explicitly) defines religion as meaningful integration of a given worldview or level (rd-2), then *the more integrative* religion (within that worldview or level) is implied or defined by the author to be the more valid. In these cases, since we refer to rd-2 as mana religion in general, we refer to its more valid forms as legitimate or "good mana" religion.

A *crisis in legitimacy* occurs whenever the prevailing mana and immortality symbols fail their integrative and defensive functions. This can occur on the lower levels of mythic-exoteric religion (for example, the Pope's encyclicals on human reproduction, based as they are on Thomistic/Aristotelian biological notions, long outmoded, have lost legitimacy with many people), on the middle levels of rational-secular religion (e.g., the Newtonian paradigm as a world view has lost legitimation), and on the upper levels of mystical religion (e.g., Mahayana Buddhism eventually lost legitimation in India, its place being taken by Shankara's Vedanta). In each case, the religion in its rd-2 function simply fails to provide enough meaningful integration, on the one hand, or enough immortality power, on the other, and thus loses its legitimacy, or its capacity to validate translation.

Corollary: "Degree of legitimacy" refers to the relative degree of integration, meaning-value, good mana, ease of functioning, avoidance of taboo, and so forth within any given level. This is a *horizontal scale;* "more legitimate" means more integrative-meaningful within that level.

9. *Authentic religion.* This is religion that primarily *validates transformation* to a particular dimension-level deemed to be most centrally religious. When an author (implicitly or explicitly) defines religion as a particular dimension-level of existence (rd-1), then the religion that more completely or accurately *contacts* that dimension-level is implied or defined by the author to be the more valid. In those cases, I use the word "authentic" or "more authentic" to indicate "more valid."

A *crisis in authenticity* occurs whenever a prevailing worldview (or religion) is faced with challenges from a *higher-level* view. This can occur at any level, whenever a new and higher (or senior) level begins to emerge and itself gain legitimacy. The new world view embodies a new and higher transformative power and thus challenges the old view, not merely as to its legitimacy but as to its very authenticity.

Corollary: "Degree of authenticity" refers to the relative degree of actual transformation delivered by a given religion (or worldview). This is a *vertical scale;* "more authentic" means more capable of reaching a higher level (and not merely integrating the present level).

An author is, of course, free to specify the nature of the centrally religious or higher realm. For myself, it is the psychic, subtle, causal, and ultimate levels of structural organization and relational exchange. It follows that, for myself, authentic religion is any practice leading to a genuine emergence of, and eventual adaptation to, those transpersonal realms (with the further understanding that causal religion is more authentic than subtle, which is more authentic than psychic). I will occasionally use the corollary "degree of authenticity" in a looser sense, as meaning the degree of developmental structuralization *in general* (e.g., myth is more authentic than magic, reason is more authentic than myth, vision is more authentic than reason, etc.). However, when I refer to authentic religions per se, they are ones that have reached a degree of structuralization at or beyond the superconscient border (i.e., psychic or higher). Thus, magic, myth, and reason can be (and often are) *legitimate* religions, and they can occasionally *express* authentic religious insight via peak experience (see chapter 6). But in neither case are they the source of *authentic* religious insight, which, for me, is always and expressly *trans*rational, not merely rational, and certainly not prerational.

Notice that, in very general terms, any religion (or world view) can be judged in its degree of validity on two different, independently variable scales: its degree of *legitimacy* (horizontal scale; degree of *translative* smoothness and integrity, measured against the potential capacity of the given level itself) and its degree of *authenticity* (vertical scale; degree of *transformative* power, measured by the degree of hierarchical structuralization delivered by the transformation). Thus, for example, there are situations where magic, at its *full* potential (say, in some paleolithic societies) was just as *legitimate* as myth at its full potential (say, in some Bronze Age societies), but myth was more *authentic* (embodying a higher level of structural organization). If our scale of legitimacy is 1 to 10 (degree of using the integrative-mana potential of the given level) and our scale of authenticity is 1 to 10 (representing the ten levels of structuralization given in figure 2), then in that example, the ratings would be (10, 4) and (10, 5), respectively. Here are some other examples, more commonplace:

Chinese Maoism has (or rather had) a fairly high degree of legitimacy but a very mediocre degree of authenticity. It was a *legitimate* religion (or worldview) in that it apparently integrated large blocks of peoples, provided social solidarity and a measure of meaning-value, and avoided a good deal of taboo by providing the immortality ideology of an unending, never-dying people's revolution (a legitimacy rating of, say, 8–9). It was not very *authentic,* however, because it offered adaptation only to or at the mythic-rational realms (5–6); say what you will, Maoism did not produce superconscient realization of, and adaptation to, only God. Thus: Maoism (8–9, 5–6). (Notice that today Maoism has lost some of its legitimacy in China; the "cultural revolution" and its subsequent events were exactly a *legitimacy crisis* as defined above.) Soviet Marxism/Leninism, on the other hand, is as inauthentic as was Maoism (5–6), for the same reasons (it does not produce psychic, subtle, or causal transformation), but it also appears to be of a much lower degree of legitimacy (say, 4–5) than Maoism in its heyday, because its mana and its immortality symbols apparently have to be backed by rather large sticks.[3] So there we have examples of relatively legitimate/inauthentic (8–9, 5–6) and illegitimate/inauthentic (4–5, 5–6). (Lest my judgment seem biased toward American-Protestant capitalism, I will quickly add that, in my opinion, the American "civil religion"—a mixture of exoteric, Protestant, biblical myths and nationalistic immortality symbols—possesses essentially the same legitimacy and authenticity ratings as did Maoism. That this civil religion faced a *legitimacy crisis* during the 1960s will be discussed in chapter 7.)

As for the authentic but illegitimate, examples abound: when Mahayana Buddhism died in India, it was not because its tenets were per se inauthentic, for they still embodied causal level practice (9–10), but because Vedanta Hinduism, regenerating itself via Shankara and claiming a more historical rootedness, became more legitimate with practitioners. Likewise, Vedanta is a perfectly causal-authentic religion, but it seems it will never achieve widespread legitimacy in America, its rating there thus being something like (1–2, 9–10). In the West, in fact, most esoteric spiritual tenets, no matter how authentic, never gained much legitimacy (witness Eckhart, al-Hallaj, Giordano Bruno, Christ's esoteric-causal message itself).

As for religions that have been both legitimate and authentic, we may take Ch'an (Zen) Buddhism during T'ang China, Vedanta Hinduism in India from the time of Gaudapada and Shankara to the British intensified occupation, or Vajrayana in Tibet from Padmasambhava to Mao Tse-tung, all of which seemed somewhere around (8–9, 9–10).

Each of the preceding nine (or more) usages of the word "religion" has its appropriate place—some "religious" expressions *are* fixation/regressions, some are immortality projects, some are mana generators, some are legitimate, some are authentic. But we must be careful to express precisely which usage we mean. Otherwise, statements such as "The religious impulse is universal," "All religions are true," "Religion is transcendental," "All religions are one at some deep level," and so on are at best strictly meaningless, at worst profoundly misleading.

6

Belief, Faith, Experience, and Adaptation

I N THIS CHAPTER I wish to distinguish religious *belief*, religious *faith*, religious (mystical or peak) *experience*, and religious structural *adaptation* (or actual adaptation to authentic-religious levels of development). For again, if they are all "religious," they are religious to differing degrees. The series itself shows increasing religious involvement: it seems you can have belief without faith, faith without experience, and experience without permanent adaptation.

BELIEF

Belief is the lowest form of religious involvement, and, in fact, it often seems to operate with no authentic religious connection whatsoever.[105] The "true believer"—one who has no literal faith, let alone actual experience—embraces a more-or-less codified belief system that appears to act most basically as a fund of immortality symbols.[10] This can be mythic-exoteric religion (e.g., fundamentalist Protestantism, lay Shintoism, pop Hinduism, etc.), rational-scientism, Maoism, civil religion, and so on. What they all have in common, when thus made a matter of "true belief," is that an ideological nexus is wedded to one's qualifications for immortality.

I believe this generates a peculiar, secondary psychodynamic: since one's immortality prospects hang on the veracity of the ideological nexus, the nexus as a whole can be critically examined only with the greatest of difficulty. Thus, when the normal and unavoidable moments of uncertainty or disbelief occur (magic: is this dance really causing rain? mythic: was the world *really* created in six days? scientistic: what happened *before* the big bang? etc.), the questioning impulses are not long allowed to remain in the self-system (they are threats to one's immortality qualifications). As a result, the disbelieving impulse tends to be *projected* onto others and then attacked "out there" with an obsessive endurance. The true believer is forever on the make, looking for converts and battling disbelievers, for, on the one hand, the mere existence of a disbeliever is one token less in the immortality account, and, on the other, if the true believer can persuade others to embrace his ideology, it helps to quiet his own disbelieving impulses. If mythic-religious, he crusades against sinners, burns witches, hangs heretics; if Marxist, he lives for the revolution that will crush disbelievers (and in the meantime jails "witches," psychiatrizes "heretics"); if scientistic, he often begins a concerted diatribe on rival (heretic) worldviews, even or especially those that are otherwise ridiculously insignificant (e.g., astrology, UFO, Uri Geller, Velikovsky, etc.). It is not the rightness or wrongness of the opposing view but the peculiar passion with which it is opposed that belies its origin: what one is trying to convert is one's own disbelieving self.

On the more benign side, belief *can* serve as the appropriate conceptual expression and codification of a religious involvement of any higher degree (faith, experience, adaptation). Here, belief system acts as a rational clarification of transrational truths, as well as the introductory, *exoteric,* preparatory "reading material" for initiates.[114] When belief systems are thus linked to actual higher (authentic) religiousness, they can be called, not because of themselves but because of association, authentic belief systems.

FAITH

Faith goes beyond belief but not as far as actual religious experience. The true believer can usually give you all the reasons he is "right," and if you genuinely question his reasons he tends to take it very personally (because you have, in fact, just questioned his qualifications for immortality). His belief system is a politics of durability. The person of faith, on the other hand, will usually have a series of beliefs, but the religious involvement of this person does not seem to be generated solely or even predominantly by the beliefs. Frequently, in fact, the person cannot say exactly why he is "right" (has faith), and should you criticize what reasons he does give, he generally takes it all rather philosophically. In my opinion this is because belief, in these cases, is not the actual source of the religious involvement; rather, the person somehow intuits very God as being immanent in (as well as transcendent to) this world and this life. Beliefs become somewhat secondary, since the same intuition can be put in any number of apparently equivalent ways ("They call Him many who is really One"). The person of faith tends to shun literalism, dogmatism, evangelicalism, fundamentalism, which define almost solely the true believer.[13]

Paradoxically, the person of faith is often in great and agonizing religious *doubt,* which the true believer rarely experiences. The true believer has projected his doubts onto others and is too busy trying to convert them to pay attention to his own inner status. The person of faith, however, begins to transcend mere consoling beliefs and thus is open to intense doubt, which the person frequently takes to be a sign of *lack* of faith, which worries him sorely. But that is not usually the case.

Here is what seems to occur: The person of faith intuits, although in a preliminary and somewhat vague fashion, the existence of very God. On the one hand, this confers a measure of peace, inner stability, and a release from mere belief. On the other hand, precisely because that is so, the person yearns for a greater closeness to this Divinity, a more complete knowledge-union with God. Since the person does not yet have this greater closeness, it throws his present state, by comparison, into *doubt* (and yearning). In fact, *the greater the faith-intuition, the greater the doubt.* Zen has a profound saying on this:

Great doubt, great enlightenment;
Small doubt, small enlightenment;
No doubt, no enlightenment.

How different that is from the literal and dogmatic certainty of the true believer.

There seem to be only two ways fundamentally to alleviate this doubt and yearning. One is to revert to mere belief and clothe the doubt in more rigid and external forms (i.e., immortality symbols). The other is to act on the yearning and advance to experience.

EXPERIENCE

Experience goes beyond faith into actual encounter and literal cognition, however brief. Experience, as I am using it, means *peak experience*,[61] a temporary insight into (and influx from) one of the *authentic* transpersonal realms (psychic, subtle, causal). In my opinion, authentic religious experience must be differentiated from mere emotional frenzy, from magical trances, and from mythic mass-enthusiasms, all of which result in a temporary suspension of reason via regression to *pre*-rational adaptations, a slide that is altogether different from *trans*-rational epiphany. Pre-rational frenzies are usually chthonic in mood, emotionally laden, body-bound, and noninsightful[105]—an emotional short-circuit that sparks and sizzles with unconscious orgiastic current. Trans-rational epiphany can be blissful, but it is also numinous, noetic, illuminative, and—most importantly—it carries a great deal of insight or understanding.[6,7]

Temporary peak experiences of the transpersonal realms can occur at almost any stage of development. Actual faith seems conducive to experience; belief systems seem to inhibit it (although none of these correlations are highly positive; peak experiences are notorious for hitting just about anybody with no apparent reason).[61] When they occur to a person who previously rejected religious involvement, such experiences might effect a "conversion," with the individual subsequently adopting a particular religious belief system in order to make sense of "what hit him" (e.g., Saint Paul).

If an authentic peak experience occurs to a mythic-religious true believer, it often has the awkward effect of energizing his or her mythic immortality symbols. The result is a "born-again" believer, a particularly explosive affair. To begin with, analytic experience[29,36] has consistently disclosed that the mythic true believer often possesses a particularly harsh superego (internalized aggression)—an *excessive* guilt, a *surplus* repression, often forged in the atmosphere of overly oppressive/puritanical parents. One of the reasons the mythic true believer might have become a true believer in the first place is to attempt to redress surplus guilt by establishing relations with a fictive-mythic parent who this time around would forgive the guilty transgressions (emotional-sexual impulses). At the same time, the unacceptable and guilty impulses can be projected as a world of *dirty* sinners out there. (I believe that is why a "sinner," in such cases, is usually two things: a disbeliever, or threat to the immortality account, and a "dirty" disbeliever, or contaminated with emotional-sexual guilt.)

When that type of belief system is hit with an authentic peak experience, the system *translates* it into the terms of its own immortality symbols. The whole ideology thus appears to receive a jolting sanctification; this allows the harsh superego to be extroverted, even more than usual, into a moralizing and proselytizing fury; and the true believer, now with the absolute approval of God Almighty Himself, sets out to remake the world in his own image. A *vertical* insight, usually yogic/saintly, is turned into a *horizontal* pitch forward, because the level of structural adaptation is incapable of containing and sustaining the cognitive flood.

On the other hand, but more rarely, an authentic peak experience might jolt a true believer into a person of faith, with subsequent diminution of particular-belief passion and opening of more universal tolerance.

The peak experience itself apparently can *originate* in any of the three higher realms of the person's as yet unrealized structural potentials—psychic, subtle, causal—with the precise nature of the experience differing in each case (panenhenic, theistic, monistic). It is also important to determine "into" which level of present structural adaptation the influx is "poured," since *that* seems to determine the form of its eventual expression—magical, mythical, rational.

Notice, then, that even with our simple scheme we have suggested nine substantially different varieties of authentic peak experience: psychic, subtle, or causal influx poured into magical, mythical, or rational structures. I believe I can produce ample *structural evidence* for each of these nine epiphanies, with the proviso that the more extreme pairings (e.g., magic with causal) are so structurally difficult to achieve that for all practical purposes they are nonexistent. Aside from that exception, examples from the other eight pairings are rather abundant. Typical shamanism, for instance, seems to be panenhenic magic, or psychic intuition poured into magic structures.[105] Beyond that, Joseph Campbell[23] has presented evidence that the *most advanced* and esoteric shamans understood that there was indeed one being behind the polyforms of naturic or panenhenic epiphanies—an example of theistic magic. Moses' Mount Sinai experience seems to have been theistic mythic, or subtle realm revelation flooding a mythic adaptation.[105] A modern-day Zen student's first major satori is monistic rational, or a causal-identity insight breaking into and through a rational adaptation.[88] Bertrand Russell's famous mystical experience appeared largely theistic rational, or subtle-realm illumination flooding logic. On the other hand, the most common form of religious/mystical experience today seems to be yogic or panenhenic rational. The individual at a rational level of adaptation gets a "peek" experience into the psychic dimension; this is often behind everything from the "aha" or "Eureka!" experience of rational scholars to the more mundane flights of ecstatic happiness that occasionally interrupt one's purposive-rational translations.[7]

Finally, there is an esoteric or highly advanced meaning of peak experience: a person already *on* the psychic level can peak experience the subtle or causal; a person on the subtle can peak the causal. This sometimes makes it very difficult to distinguish yogic, saintly, and sagely religions, because occasionally all three will claim that all things are mere modifications of a radiant One Reality, but only the latter claims it as matter of enduring structural adaptation, the others basing the claim on mere peak experience.[7,22,105] We will now investigate that distinction.

STRUCTURAL ADAPTATION

A peak experience, however authentic, is nonetheless merely a glimpse into those transpersonal realms that can be actually and permanently realized via higher *transformative growth* and actual structural adaptation.[101] We will, in this section, examine the implications of that view.

Prior to the modern-day influx of Eastern religions to the West, most religious scholars, psychologists, and sociologists tended to look at religion solely in terms of belief and/or faith. Largely through the influence of Eastern religion, but also due to an increased interest in Christian mysticism, Neoplatonism, and so on, the idea of *actual religious experience* (usually mystical) was added to belief and faith.

In some ways the psychologists led the field in this exploration. William James's *Varieties* was a classic investigation that concluded that the fundamental wellspring of religion was neither belief nor faith but direct experience. After all, he noted, all world religions *began* as an experience in some prophet/seer and only later were codified into belief systems that demanded faith. Carl Jung directed his investigations to the possible archetypal wellsprings of such experience, and then—relatively recently—Maslow's studies made *peak experience* the fundamental paradigm of authentic religiosity.

It has been a mixed blessing. However appropriate and necessary the peak paradigm was in helping scholars see beyond belief and faith to direct experience, the paradigm itself has blinded us to the fact that actual adaptation to these higher realms is a permanent and stable possibility and not merely a fleeting experience. A person can evolve to, for example, the saintly level of structural adaptation with the same eventual stability and continuous functioning that a person can now operate at the linguistic level.[101] We do not speak of such stable adaptations as "experiences," just as we do not say, of the typical person, "He's having a linguistic experience"—he is *at* the linguistic level, *as* that level, more or less continuously.

Once we see that, beyond mere transitory experience, authentic religiosity might actually involve concrete developmental transformation and structural adaptation, then we introduce a revolution in the cognitive validity of spiritual knowledge and truth-claims. For mere belief cannot be cognitively verified, since it has no manifest referent; nor can faith, since it has no necessary content. Consequently, when psychologists and theologians introduced mystical *experience,* they thought they finally had a way to verify or cognitively ground religious claims, because experience is at least concrete. Unfortunately, it is also transitory, fleeting, impossible to replicate, privatistic, and altogether too brief to establish any claim to cognitive validity, as philosophers were very happy (and very correct) to explain.

On the other hand, if we understand that yogic, saintly, and sagely knowledge-claims are based, *not* on belief, faith, or transitory experience, but on actual levels of structuralization, cognition, and development, then the deep structures of their truth-claims assume a perfectly appropriate, verifiable, and replicable status. In fact, they would assume precisely the same *type* of status as, for example, Piaget's levels and Kohlberg's stages and could be clearly demonstrated so in the same basic way: via stage-structural analyses in any correspondingly adapted community of adequately evolved practitioners. (We will return to this topic in chapter 9.)

I realize that the theologians are just now moving from belief and faith to experience, a move that is generating much excitement, enthusiasm, and controversy.* While all of that is a step in the right direction, I feel that its severe limitations should be kept in mind and that we should move on, as quickly as possible, from the paradigm of peak experience to the paradigm of structural adaptation.

---

* Witness Peter Berger's *The Heretical Imperative.*

7

Present-Day Sociology of Religion

W ITH THE ABOVE as background, we can quickly make a few schematic comments on various theories and topics now at the forefront of the sociology of religion.

INCREASING RATIONALISM

Sociologists since Weber have been interested in the increasing trend toward secularization, individualism, and rationalism. In the face of the increasingly purposive-rational worldviews, the older mythological worldviews, based primarily on exoteric mythic-membership and traditional conformity, began slowly but inevitably to lose their cogency, and the very process of legitimation began to shift, in every sector, to rational adjudication and humanistic-secular appropriation. This process is far from complete, and most cultures have yet a way to go before the integrative-stabilizing forces inherent in the rational level of adaptation and organization achieve anything resembling their structural potential. But I am convinced that the mythic-membership structure has reached the inherent limit of its integrative and truth-disclosing capacities. It first emerged c. 9000 B.C. in certain mythic farming cultures, where it slowly replaced the paleolithic magic of the great hunt; it matured in the high civilizations of classic mythology (Egypt, Shang China, Indus Valley India); and it peaked in medieval Europe under mythic-exoteric Christianity.[105] It began to die in seventeenth-century Europe; each succeeding decade has been largely defined by those persons and events that disclosed the mythic inadequacy and made plain its obsolescence: Copernicus, Newton, Locke, Nietzsche, Comte, Darwin, Freud, and so on. There are and will certainly continue to be repressions/fixations to this mode, both in individuals and societies at large, but in my opinion its force as a cogent and legitimating *translator of reality* is defunct. It can no longer provide mana of a high enough degree, and few educated individuals *can* believe its mythic immortality symbols. Like all levels of structural adaptation, it is phase-specific. Its leading-edge phase has passed (which does not prevent it from being dominant in prerational pockets of culture here and abroad).

Thus, I agree with sociologists in general that the central course of modern development is marked by increasing rationalization. However, my major point is that the overall trend of rationalization only covers the *first half* of our proposed developmental scheme: archaic to magic to mythic to rational. But the scheme *continues* from rational to psychic to subtle to causal to ultimate, and thus what perhaps distinguishes my viewpoint from other spiritually sympathetic theorists is that I believe the trend of rationalization per se is necessary, desirable, appropriate, phase-specific, and evolutionary. In fact, I believe it is therefore perfectly religious, *in and by itself* (no matter how apparently secular), in sense rd-4: an expression of increasingly advanced consciousness and articulated awareness that has as its final aim, and itself contributes to, the resurrection of Spirit.

I also believe rational adaptation is perfectly religious in sense rd-2: capable of providing a legitimate, cogent, integrative, and meaningful worldview, or good mana (rd-8). Now, it cannot provide us with a Total Worldview—only causal/ultimate impact, according to the sages, can achieve absolutization.[7] But it can, I believe, provide a worldview every bit as coherent and meaningful as archaic magic or syncretic myth—more so, in my opinion, for reasons we will soon investigate.

But the form of rational-individual integration is so different from that of mythic-conformity that it sometimes confuses scholars. Mythic-membership is marked by an intermediate degree of perspectivism: greater than magic, which has almost none, but not as developed as rational-reflexive, which is the first major structure to display easy and continuous perspectivism. Perspectivism itself is simply the capacity to *take the role of others,* to cognitively project oneself into a mental perspective and viewpoint other than one's own. Psychologists from Werner to Piaget have demonstrated how and why increasing perspectivism, or conversely, decreasing egocentricism, is a primary indicator of development.[57,70,95] Mythic-membership ranks intermediate; it is aware of others, and can begin to take the role of others, but because it is something of a learner's stage in perspectivism, it tends to become trapped in those roles, defined by those roles, bound to them. It is thus captured by a conformist, conventional, or traditional attitude: the culture's codes are its codes, the society's norms are its norms, what they want is what I want. This is exactly Kohlberg's conventional and Loevinger's conformist stages.

With the rise of rational level, however, the person moves into a more self-and-other reflexive, or perspectivist, position. The person can, for the first time, critically distance himself from society's norms and thus adjudicate them for himself. He can norm the norms. He might find them unworthy and reject them; he might find them honorable and embrace them, but in either case he does so out of potentially reasonable and perspectivist considerations, and no longer out of blind conformity. This, of course, is Kohlberg's postconventional and Loevinger's conscientious-individualistic stages.

The paradigm of mythic-membership unity seems to be "Everybody has to think the same thing, share the same symbols, and have the same father-god-king in common." The paradigm of rational-individual unity seems to be "Let's do different things together, share different symbols, exchange different perspectives." That is still a perfectly *legitimate* form of integration or social stability; it simply does not cater to the conformity-traditional paradigm, which many sociologists seem to take as sacred. Its stability does not depend upon mythic mana, or exchange of conformity units, but on rational mana, or exchange of self-reflexive units. Mythic-membership achieves unity via shared belongingness needs; rational-individual, via shared self-esteem needs (to use Maslow's needs hierarchy). In many ways, it is potentially *more* stabilizing than mythic-membership translation because it is more resilient, more *differentiated* and *therefore* more potentially integrated. For developmental theorists, differentiation and integration are not opposites, they are complements, as when Werner summarizes: "Wherever development occurs it proceeds from a state of relative globality and lack of differentiation to a state of increasing differentiation, articulation, and hierarchical integration." Rational-individuation stands in just that relationship to the globality of mythic-membership, and it is that fact that allows scholars such as Fenn[30] and Bell[12] to point out that modern society can potentially achieve adequate stabilization without recourse to fused traditionalistic units of mana. Ogilvy's *Many Dimensional Man* presents a persuasive (although very phase-specific) argument for perspectivist integrity, or unity *via* diversity, which he contrasts with the older but once appropriate integrity of one-god, one-king, one-party mentality.

If individuals at the rational level of structural adaptation choose then to pursue an *authentic* religion, as opposed to the merely *legitimate* religion of secular-rationalism, they almost invariably carry their perspectivism with them and acknowledge that there are different but equally valid approaches to authentic religion—so unlike the mythic-membership believer, who, lacking sophisticated perspectivism, usually claims that his father-god-king is the only possible one and that if you want to get saved, you "got to get" membership.*

At the same time, I do not want to glorify the rational-individual level of adaptation. It is merely phase-specific. I believe it too will pass, eventually to be subsumed in a truly yogic worldview. We may further suppose that, like any level, it can translate its world sanely or morbidly, provide good mana or bad. There seems to be "good" and "bad" reason just as there is "good" and "bad" mythology. But in my opinion we should not take the worst of reason, compare it with the best of mythology, and then claim reason itself, or the level of differentiated-individuated rational adaptation, is a degenerate structure in contrast to yesterday's "really religious," Garden-of-Eden, mythic-conformity modes.

My point is that religious scholars have often seen the trend toward rationalization and concluded that it is an anti-religious trend, whereas for me it is a *pro-authentic-religious* trend by virtue of being transmythic or post-mythic and *on its way to* yogic and higher levels of structural adaptation. If indeed rationality is the great divide between subconscient magic and myth and superconscient subtle and causal, then its major purpose in the overall scheme of evolution might be to strip Spirit of its infantile and childish associations, parental fixations, wish fulfillments, dependency yearnings, and symbiotic gratifications. When Spirit is thus de-mythologized, it can be approached *as* Spirit, in its Absolute Suchness (*tathata*), and not as a Cosmic Parent.

When asked to explain the religious worldview that rationalization is supposedly "destroying," such scholars almost always point to magic or mythic symbologies, thereby elevating prerational structures to a trans-

---

*For an excellent discussion of modern sociological pluralism/perspectivism, see Berger's *The Heretical Imperative*.

rational status. Since development *does* move from prerational myth to rational discourse to transrational epiphany,[102] then if one confuses authentic religion with myth, naturally rationalization *appears* anti-religious. If, however, authentic religion is seen to be transrational, then the phase-specific moment of rational-individuation is not only a step in the right direction, it is an absolutely necessary prerequisite.

ROBERT BELLAH

In my opinion, the greatest contribution of Bellah's work, other than being marked at every turn by immense clarity and perception, is his rigorous demonstration that in some sense religion should be treated as religious, that is, nonreductionistically. This started a minor revolution in modern sociology. Beyond that, however, I have a few reservations.*

1. In treating all religious expressions "nonreductionistically," Bellah tends to lose any serious critical capacity (see chapter 1, section C, Phenomenological-Hermeneutics). Indeed, when he says "religion is true," he abandons the position of *profound* developmental possibilities and overlooks the hierarchy of truth capacities. One might as well say "morality is true" and then overlook the extraordinary differences— including the increasingly *higher* nature—of the half-dozen or so stages of moralization discovered by modern developmental psychology.

This lack of vertical critical dimension, under what often seems to me a questionable use of "nonreductionism," not only overlooks the possible hierarchy of authentic religious adaptation—yogic, saintly, sagely—it takes at close to face value any apparently religious symbol ("symbolic realism") and thus accords eminent status to what might simply be childish fixations. Reductionism, in my opinion, rightly refers to trying to explain *higher* domains by *lower* ones (mind by instinct, subtle by mind, etc.), and that is indeed deplorable. Bellah, however, does not systematically distinguish higher and lower; reductionism thus comes to mean saying anything about a domain other than what it wishes to say about itself. Especially, Bellah does not distinguish prerational religion from transrational religion and thus, in trying to protect the latter from reductionism, he often must glorify the former.

---

* [See *Sex, Ecology, Spirituality* for a discussion of Bellah's important contributions in elucidating the evolutionary-structural stages of religion. See also "Sociocultural Evolution," in volume 4 of the *Collected Works*, for a discussion of other aspects of Bellah's works.]

2. Bellah's background definition of religion is that which serves the holistic interrelation of subject and object in a meaningful way. This is basically rd-2: religion as the relational exchange of mana (on whatever level). It is with this definition that Bellah can (correctly) say that all societies are religious, even secular ones, and that all religions (in that sense) are true. And because he is generally working with rd-2, his criteria of "more valid" religion is rd-8: a more integrative religion is a more valid, useful, or meaningful one. The criterion here is that of *legitimacy*. For example, the American "civil religion" (a mixture of mythic Protestant ethic and American nationalistic immortality symbols) is or was a legitimate religion, according to Bellah, because it provided adequate integrative-meaning, moral restraint, and social cohesion. I agree that that is so. The civil religion was a good mana generator and taboo avoider; it was a legitimate religion (in the rd-8 sense).

However, because of his noncritical ("nonreductionistic") stance, Bellah fails to distinguish systematically between such merely legitimate religions and *authentic* religions. Thus, he will say things like, "The civil religion at its best is a *genuine apprehension of universal and transcendental reality*. . . ."[13] Now, say what you will, civil religion per se, even at its best, did not produce anything resembling real satori, moksha, or *genuine apprehension* of very Spirit. This obfuscation occurs, in my opinion, because Bellah confuses legitimate mana religion—what should happen on all levels of structural adaptation—with authentic-transcendent religion, which happens only on the upper levels of structural adaptation.

3. On occasion, however, Bellah will also use religion as rd-1; for various reasons, he has a specific dimension-realm in mind when he says "religion," and that realm, whatever else it is, is not scientific-rational. Thus he will say, "It is in this sense religious, not scientific."[13] That is a perfectly acceptable usage of religion, as we have seen; it is rd-1.

In my opinion, Bellah is here attempting to refer not merely to a *legitimate* religion, which even secular-rational society can be, but also to an *authentic* religion, which is beyond or trans to rational-individuation (and which, therefore, Bellah is understandably reluctant to grant to scientific-secular societies; in my view, they may be legitimate but are not authentic). But in failing systematically to distinguish between transrational and prerational domains, Bellah extends *authenticity* to prerational, mythic engagements and civil religions, whereas they possessed at most a sturdy *legitimacy*. Now scientific-rational society is, for a variety of reasons, today facing various sorts of legitimation crises itself, and these are an important topic of investigation and criticism. But I believe that Bellah confuses the present-day loss of legitimation, which civil and mythic religions had, with a loss of *authenticity* that they *never* possessed. He thus laments: "So-called postreligious man, the cool, self-confident secular man that even some theologians have recently celebrated, is trapped in a literal and circumscribed reality that is classically described in religious terms as the world of death and sin, the fallen world, the world of illusion. Postreligious man is trapped in hell."[13]

What Bellah calls "postreligious" is simply postmythic and postconventional. And, as we suggested in the last section, postmythic men and women are not post-authentic-religious, but preauthentic-religious, poised at the rational level of structural adaptation, ready for the next overall step in collective development and the *first* step in authentic, collective, spiritual experience—that of widespread yogic adaptation. Trapped in hell? Most definitely, as are *all* stages short of superconscient resurrection. But the point is that the previous mythic-religious men and women were equally trapped in hell—in fact, more so; they simply had not the high degree of rational-reflexive awareness necessary to thoroughly realize their plight, and thus suffered their misery in relative innocence, allowing what qualms as might surface to be suckled by a mythic cosmic parent. *That* covenant needed to be broken.

They are indeed still trapped in hell, as were their predecessors, but postmythic men and women have at least, and finally, thrown off their childish images of deity as a protective parent sniveling over their every move, listening to their every wish-fulfillment, catering to their every immortality project, dancing to their prayers of magic. Postmythic men and women did not get thrown out of Eden; they grew up and walked out, and, in now assuming rational and personal responsibility for a measure of their own lives, stand preparatory for the next great transformation: the God within, not the Father without.

4. Finally, Bellah maintains that religion, unlike science, has no verifiable (testable) cognitive truth-claim. I disagree with this strongly, for reasons suggested in chapter 6 and discussed again in chapter 9.

ANTHONY AND ROBBINS

Dick Anthony and Thomas Robbins have recently moved to correct what they see as some of the weaknesses and contradictions in Bellah's theories, principally by replacing (or supplementing) symbolic realism with structuralism, and specifically a structuralism modeled on Chomsky's deep and surface patterns.

I am obviously in sympathy with the main thrust of their work, and I can recommend its general features with enthusiasm. Here, I would simply like to suggest a few minor amendments to their presentations in light of our discussion thus far.

1. Anthony and Robbins[3] begin by suggesting that Bellah's approach to religion, which sees it as a universal and nonreducible *factum* of human existence, is a start toward a long-sought formulation of "universal structural principles intrinsic to religion," that is, "Symbolic realism seems to imply a fundamental unity of all religions at a deep level." They point out, however, that Bellah fails to carefully distinguish between the deep structures of such universal religion, which would be largely invariant and ahistorical, and the surface structures of religion, which would be mostly variable and contingent. Consequently, they note, "Bellah's recent work has emphasized two trends that, on the face of it, seem contradictory. In his metatheoretical papers, he has stressed the underlying uniformity of seemingly diverse religious traditions and epochs. However, in his actual description of concrete religious systems, Bellah has emphasized the necessity of religious change [and] religious evolution. . . ." Anthony and Robbins then argue that

> the apparent contradictions between these positions arise because Bellah has not made explicit the distinction between the surface structure and deep structure of religions. When he emphasizes the similarities in religions of different cultures and epochs, he is focusing upon what should properly be called the deep structure of religion. When he focuses upon the changes in religion relative to changing psychological, sociological, and economic conditions, he is describing surface structures.

As cogent as that argument for deep and surface structure is (we will return to it in a moment), the failure to make that distinction is not primarily the cause of "the apparent contradictions" in Bellah's work. Bellah does not, it is true, explicitly make that important distinction, but *prior* to that omission, in my opinion, is the more fundamental lack of distinction between legitimate and authentic religions, *each* class of which has representative deep and surface features. For example, there is the deep structure of magic religion (marked by confusion of symbol and thing symbolized, condensation, diplacement, etc.), and there are actual surface manifestations of magic religion (voodoo here, naturic animism there, Bon religion here, and so on). There is the deep structure of causal religion (marked by unmanifest absorption, identity of self and absolute ground, etc.), and there are actual surface manifestations of causal religion (Zen, Vedanta, Eckhart, etc.). And so with each class. If these levels of structural realization are not first distinguished, then any merely legitimate religion may be confused with genuinely authentic religion, and the *dynamics* of legitimacy may be likewise confused with the *dynamics* of authenticity. That is, what happens at each level of the spectrum of existence (universal or ever-present need for mana, meaning) might be confused with what specifically defines the *higher* levels of the spectrum (actual universal mysticism), with the result that what we mean by "deep" and "surface" structures is skewed from the start, most often by having "deep" mean authentic (or mystical) and "surface" mean legitimate, instead of seeing that authentic religions have deep and surface structures, legitimate religions have deep and surface structures, and the two do not necessarily overlap.

Let me give as a correlative example Maslow's work on the hierarchy of needs, which are: physiological needs (material), safety needs (magic-body protective), belongingness needs (mythic-membership), self-esteem needs (rational-reflexive), self-actualization needs (centaur/psychic), and the self-transcendence needs (subtle/causal).[61] Now we can say *need is universal,* or ever-present, which of course it is, because it occurs on *all* levels. But that "need-as-universal" is not to be confused with *the* need for universal-mystical self-transcendence, which occurs on the *highest* levels. Just so, if we define religion as meaning-need (rd-2), then of course it is universal and occurs on all levels, as mana search, and we can further investigate what constitutes *good* mana on all levels (rd-8), so as to trace out the actual *dynamics* and possible functional invariants, cross-level, of legitimation itself. But if by religion we *also* wish somehow to convey, as Anthony and Robbins appropriately do, a meaning of authentic or universal-mystical union (and *philosophia perennis*), then only the highest and transcendent levels are directly involved.

Those are two completely different (but equally important) forms of "universal religiousness" or "universal structural principles intrinsic to religion," principally because they reflect two quite different forms of religion (rd-2 and rd-1) and correlative validity scales (rd-8 and rd-9, or legitimacy and authenticity). The former is a universality of all good-mana religion at some deep level, "deep level" here meaning the functional similarities and dynamics of all legitimately integrative-horizontal translations. The latter is a "transcendental unity" reached and shared only by those rather rare sub-sects of certain religions that actually embrace an authentically mystical or *esoteric* level, or the superconscient realm in general, which is what scholars of the *philosophia perennis* mean by the phrase "transcendent unity of religions." Bellah's work deals basically with the former, or legitimate mana and taboo-avoidance (or accumulation of immortality symbols, which is why I think he speaks so highly of Norman O. Brown's works). Anthony and Robbins wish to make more explicit room for the latter, or authentic mystical religion, but—in failing to explicitly distinguish legitimate and authentic—they generally try to make the former a surface structure of the latter as deep structure. They consequently overlook the possibility that mysticism per se (panenhenic, theistic, or monistic) is the deep structure of which *only* the authentic religions (yogic, saintly, or sagely) are surface structures. For, in my opinion, actual mysticism is no more the deep structure of, for example, civil religion, than the self-transcendence need is the deep structure of, for example, the safety needs.

In other words, Anthony and Robbins significantly improve Bellah's ideas by introducing deep and surface structures to his formulations, but they tend to simply reproduce his confusion of legitimate and authentic religions, the confusion of legitimate mana on any level with authentic mana on the mystical levels, the confusion of universal functional invariants of good integration with universal mystical integration. They then take the deep structure of authentic mysticism (or divine immanence) and instead of assigning it its own *authentic* surface structures, assign it any merely *legitimate* surface structures from any lower level, no matter how otherwise completely lacking in authenticity they might be. It is in this vein that they say, for example, "Maoism shares certain universal features of traditional religions (and thus *is* a religion in our sense), whereas Russian communism does not. . . ."[3] These features, which Maoism supposedly possesses, Anthony and Robbins wish explicitly to connect to the deep structure of "an inner experience of ultimate reality."[3] In other words, the deep structure of authentic mysticism is supposed to underlie the surface structure of legitimate Maoism. Again, I think it is obvious that the experience of Maoism and the experience of samadhi are not related as surface and deep structures but as two different levels of structuralization altogether. Better to say that Maoism is a *legitimate* religion (surface structure) at the mythic-to-rational level (deep structure), whereas Russian communism is still struggling for similar legitimacy at the same level, but *neither* are *authentic* religions, as are, for example, Vedanta and Zen, which are two different but more or less legitimate surface structures (in India and Japan, respectively) of the *same* causal-level deep structure.

At the same time, one can compare all types of *legitimate* religions, whether also authentic or not—say, Maoism, American civil religion, Vajrayana in precommunistic Tibet, exoteric Shi'ite Islam—in order to determine what they have in common ("deep structure" in an entirely different sense) as good integrators of societies, and thus discover and formulate the dynamics and basic functional invariants of "healthy" religion. I have already suggested that such dynamics would include good mana production and taboo avoidance (via meaning-units and immortality symbols). Such "deep structures," in their potential form, would also probably be native, as explained for translative potentials in chapter 4. Lack of authenticity would then be related to lack of *transformative* symbology; lack of legitimacy, to lack of adequate *translative* symbology, itself related in part to a failure of transcription, or adequate read-out of the potentials available to the particular level.

In summary, if the distinction deep/surface is made without the prior distinction of authentic/legitimate, then one of the results is that *authentic* mysticism may appear to be the deep structure of which all lower and merely *legitimate* religions are supposed to be surface structures, instead of seeing that each level has its own deep and surface structures, that the surface structures can function legitimately or illegitimately on every level, that only on the highest levels does authentic mystical union manifest itself, and that the deep structures of those mystical levels— psychic, subtle, causal—have as surface structures only the religions evoking them—yogic, saintly, sagely.

2. Anthony, in an important paper ("A Phenomenological-Structuralist Approach to the Scientific Study of Religion"),[2] the merits of which I will emphasize in a moment, again suggests "convergence of lines of evidence pointing toward *universal mysticism* as the data base for the deep structure component of . . . a two-level [deep/surface] structuralist theory of religion." Now we have already suggested that universal mysticism is *not* the deep structure of lower-level legitimate religions, such as magic-voodoo, exoteric mythic religion, Maoism, or civil religion, for they take as deep structure the intrinsic rules and patterns that define and govern the particular (lower) level of structural adaptation on which their existence is grounded.

But what I wish specifically to emphasize in this section is that even when we understand that actual mysticism is the deep structure of only authentic religious experience-adaptation, we still have to be careful to differentiate the hierarchical *types* of mystical union. There are at least three or four types, as we have seen, and each has a *deep structure* (psychic, subtle, causal, or ultimate) that underlies various *surface structures* of authentic religious symbology (e.g. and respectively, Tundra Shamanism, Mosaic Judaism, Vedanta Hinduism, Maha Ati Vajrayana), authentic religious practice (e.g. and respectively, hatha-yoga arousal, shabd or interior prayer-contemplation, jnana-insight or radical absorption in the Heart, and sahaja or ultimate-spontaneous Identity), and authentic mystical unions (panenhenic, theistic, monistic, nondual).

My own feeling is that even this four-level hierarchy will soon be replaced with a much more complex one, containing up to a dozen discrete developmental structures. But in any event, the old notion that there are only two types or levels of religion—exoteric, which is everywhere different, and esoteric, which is everywhere identical—is about as precise as saying there are two forms of mental cognition, primary and secondary. That early Freudian division is acceptable enough, but we can be much more precise: for example, Piaget's description of four structure-stages, which is, of course, exactly the type of refinement I believe will happen with both exoteric *and* esoteric religions.

But the real reason I mention Anthony's paper is that, aside from these small amendments, I believe it is packed with all the right insights and suggestions for a general structural approach to religion. There is no need of my merely repeating his contributions here; I suggest the reader consult the paper itself, for the essentials of his suggestions are surely ones we will want to include in a well-rounded approach to religion.

3. The refinements I have suggested might also allow us to tease apart the idea that only surface structures change in religious history while deep structures remain everywhere monolithic. Now it is true that a deep structure in itself is a-historical, but it *emerges* in the course of history, and we can trace those revolutionary emergences. On the other hand, when it is thought that there is only *one* basic deep structure of religion, then naturally that deep structure must also be assumed to have been present from the earliest religious expression, and so all religious history is pictured as a mere shuffling of various surface structures around this "single," "universal" deep structure. But once we see that there might be four or more major deep structures of authentic religion

(not to mention exoteric religions), then it becomes more than probable that the history of religion involves not only evolution of surface structures but also revolution in deep structures.

Stated differently, most religions, in the course of their histories, seem to face various *legitimation crises,* usually prompted by various rival surface structures. But occasionally a particular religion might face what amounts to an *authentication crisis*: it either fails to provide the actual *transformation* that it promised, or it is faced with a religion that delivers higher-level transformation altogether. For example, at least two such significant transformations in the West seem to have occurred:[105] (1) The transformation from a somewhat crude yogic-shamanistic and panenhenic worship to a truly subtle and saintly involvement, epitomized perhaps by Moses, who, according to legend, descended from Mount Sinai to directly challenge such "nature worship"; and (2) the transformation from Mosaic saintly worship to causal identity, epitomized by Christ and al-Hallaj, both of whom were murdered "because you, being a man, make yourself out God."

These religion-transformational crises and conflicts are, I believe, simply a subset of what happens at every level of development as a new and higher structure emerges to replace or subsume the prior and lower. My point is simply that, in the study of religious development (as a subset of general developmental principles), we might be sensitive to the differences in historico-dynamics between surface structure rivalries and deep structure revolutions, between legitimation crises and authentication crises.

THE NEW RELIGIONS

There is an abundance of literature dealing with the new religious movements in America; they seem to be the acid test of a sociological theory. In this section I will apply the theory of transcendental sociology in outline form.

1. We can again begin with Bellah's work, for I think his analysis of American civil religion is cogent. I disagree that it was an authentic religion, but it seemed most definitely a legitimate religion: it served good mana on a mythic-membership level and it offered an easy abundance of taboo-avoidance and immortality symbols. According to Bellah (and others), the American civil religion fatally hemorrhaged in the 1960s,

and the new religions, in various forms, are in large measure the result. What follows—the rest of section 1—is my *opinion* of what happened.

The old civil-religious, traditional-membership covenant was already under strain due to increasing rationalization and consequent (healthy) de-mythologizing; what legitimation it had left was finally broken under the combined onslaught of radical student politics, post-conventional rationality, Vietnam, alternative (Eastern) spiritual epiphanies, economic doubts, and a general debunking of American nationalism. As the old translation-covenant finally disintegrated, it left in its wake *three separate lines of development,* lines that were already in existence to some degree but now stood naked in their form and accelerated in their pace.

a. The sector of ongoing secular-rationalization, which has now dominated the universities, the media, most central political-technical steering decisions, the intelligentsia, and the worldview of most educated, liberal individuals.

b. A very small sector that, already brought up in an atmosphere of increasing rational-secularism and more or less adapted to it, began to search for, or actually develop to, transrational and transpersonal structuralization. Interest in Eastern yogic and meditative disciplines, Christian and Jewish mysticism, and certain new forms of intensive psychotherapy, were evidence of a thirst for such transrational saturation. *However,* not all, not even most, individuals interested in the "new religions" were authentically ready for actual transrational and yogic adaptation, because . . .

c. The broken covenant found a large sector of the population unready and unable to transform to responsible, postmythic, rational individuality (let alone transrational yogic discipline). This was exacerbated by the uncontested fact that the (horizontal) developmental course of rational-individuation was not itself operating up to its integrative potential: it was not providing the good mana it is structurally capable of. Thus, for various reasons, a significant number of individuals were alienated from the rational-individual society that was rapidly if precariously emerging. In search of some sort of legitimate mana (integrative truth), some of these individuals took regressive consolation in various prerational immortality symbols and mythological ideologies. These were largely of two sorts.

(1) Fundamentalistic mythic religion: a new surge in exoteric Protestant mythology, complete with proselytizing fury, evangelical non-

perspectivism, saved-by-the-father (Oedipal) immortality symbols, patriarchal sexism, and authoritarian obedience. Largely composed of true believers, this sector, basically, wanted to put the broken covenant back together again.

(2) Cultic new age religions: such as the Moonies, Hare Kirshna, Jesus freaks, and so forth; these are essentially *identical* in deep structure with the fundamentalist mythic religion of the evangelicals, but their drastically different surface structures have the all-important advantage of allowing one, in such cults, to express disaffection with both rational society *and* one's parents, should one's parents already be expressing disaffection with rationality via mythic revivals. Dressing up like a Hindu can both scream disapproval of society at large and really get to your own fundamentalist Christian parents; even better, dress up like Jesus Christ.

My point is simply that "the" new religions really involve at least two drastically different structural celebrations: transrational, on the one hand, and prerational, on the other. The former is primarily (but not solely) a manifestation of ongoing postrational development, vertical transformation, and higher structuralization, whereas the latter is largely (but not solely) a product of failure at rational-individuation (exposed when the covenant broke) and a regression/fixation to prerational, mythic, and even archaic-magical (narcissistic) structural disadvantages, which define much of the "new age" movements.[102]

2. There remains the possible role that the authentic mystical sector (*b* above) might have in actual large-scale societal transformation. For our general paradigm of revolutionary (not merely evolutionary) change is as follows: the present translation begins to fail its soothing, phase-specific integrative tasks, that is, its units of meaning no longer command common sense; too many of its immortality symbols have shockingly suffered damage (death); structural tension begins to increase, driving the system into various turmoils and perturbations; the structure eventually begins to loosen and break; if there are no viable seed crystals in the old translative repertoire, the system either regresses to lower forms or completely disintegrates; if there are viable seed crystals, then the structural tensions are absorbed and channeled through those crystals, and the system as a whole escapes its conflicts into a higher level of structural organization and integration. The old translation dies; transformation ensues; new and higher translations are born.

So where do we look for these seed crystals? Where are the enclaves and harbingers of future transformation? By definition-paradigm, they are most likely in those sectors now deemed "out-law" by the laws and in-laws of the present translation. Robbins and Anthony[77] quote Tiryakian:

> If we accept the notion that social revolutions essentially involve a fundamental re-ordering of the social structure, and if we accept the supposition that the social order is essentially viewed as a moral phenomenon by the members of the collectivity, then there must be a new source of morality involved in societal change, one that both desacralizes the present system and paves the way for the acceptance of a new order. (This is the death and rebirth aspect of social revolutions [we have already examined this death/rebirth aspect of all forms of transformation; see chapter 4, "Transformation"].) Since established religion represents a compromise with the ongoing secular institutions, the only other possible host of revolutionary thought, however unwittingly, is the noninstitutionalized religious sector. . . .

Thus, concludes Tiryakian, "important ideational components of change (i.e., changes in the social consciousness of reality) may often originate in the noninstitutionalized ["out-law"] groups or sectors of society whose paradigms of reality may, in certain historical moments, become those which replace institutionalized paradigms and become in turn new social blueprints."

I believe such statements are true, but it would help if we could be more specific. For notice that although all future truths are now contained in out-laws (by definition), not all out-laws are truthful (just as in science only the theories that today seem absurd *can* be the truths of tomorrow, but not all absurd theories are therefore true—most are, in fact, absurd, today and tomorrow). Just so with social "absurdities": in the class of general out-laws in any society, there are prelaws, counter-laws, and translaws, and apparently their influences on social revolutions are completely different.

Pre-laws are those individuals who, for various reasons, are not able or do not wish to rise to the average expectable level of structural adaptation of a given society. They often end up in jails (as blatant anti-laws) or mental institutions, although frequently their preconventional structuralization is benign enough and simply adds, for want of a better metaphor, salt to societal stew. But it should be noted that *most* of the teachings and practices that call themselves "esoteric" or "occult" are, in my opinion, prelaw; they are thinly rationalized magic, *not* psychic and *not* saintly. Astrology, tarot, "magick," voodoo, festival ritual, and such largely follow exactly the deep structure of magical/primary process cognition, and they—along with other forms of prelaw, preconventional consciousness—are *not* seed crystals of the future, unless that future spells regression.

Counter-laws make up the largest portion of what is loosely called "counterculture." Neither prelaw nor translaw, counter-law is the precise mirror image of the present law. It is largely composed of adolescent-like mentality, which, in a phase-specifically appropriate enough fashion, attempts to establish individual identities by taking each facet of present law and either acting out its precise *converse* (e.g., short-hair society produces long-hair counterculture) or its precise *caricature* (prove mastery of it and thus independence from it by "hamming it up," although this is initially an unconscious posturing and thus is performed with monumental seriousness; e.g., Mom and Dad drink, I'll be a drunk). If either of these tendencies is overblown, the counter-law becomes an anti-law (and is usually jailed). In general, however, "Counterculture may be described," says Marin, "as the tribalized, ritualized, mirror of national culture."[59]

Notice in particular that when authentic yogic-saintly religions are introduced to counter-laws, those disciplines are merely *translated* into the terms of the struggle for adaptation at adolescent rationality (i.e., counter-rationality). Such otherwise authentic disciplines thus end up embodying, via caricature, all of the predominant values of the present laws and translations of society. In this particular case, "New spiritual patterns, like the sixties counterculture, do not really challenge or antithesize dominant cultural patterns, but rather reflect and elaborate those patterns, including consumerism, individualism, spiritual privitism, and a fetishism of 'techniques.' "[77] Counter-laws can take authentic spiritual practices and turn them into caricatured thrills, "so self-centered," says Bellah, "that they begin to approximate the consumer cafeteria model."[78]

This is not to say these counter-law movements are therefore trivial; they are not transformative, but they do seem to serve a useful function for *present* society: they help forward and stabilize the given translations of the society by allowing its members, especially adolescent-phasers, to embrace its dominant values while pretending not to, thus accomplishing necessary socialization and individuation at once. In allowing its counter-laws to stand out in theory, it tucks them in in fact. Failure to grasp that elemental point has led more than one scholar to mistake counter-laws for translaws and proclaim the greening of America, the aquarian new age, and so on.

So far, we have discussed prelaws and counter-laws (and possible anti-laws): The prelaws are a relatively regressive sector, either trapped in or exploiting levels of structural organization lower than the present, average expectable level of societal translation. Their effect is per se disintegrative; however, in small numbers, and especially in their more benign modes, they may contribute to the overall translative integration of society by forming sub-societies that answer their own needs and thus spare society the disruption. Should this sector assume significant proportions, however, it generally becomes a source (or a symptom) of what can only be called "decadence," and if society at large finds its own higher-level translations burdensome, a truly disintegrative-regressive trend can result. The classic example, apparently, is Rome.

The counter-laws, on the other hand, usually serve the overall translative integration of society by embracing its fundamental values via a converse-caricatured rehearsal that simultaneously allows the necessary process of individuation and post-conformist moralization. This seems to be the basis of the swing in styles with each generation; Eisenhower parents produced student radicals who now, as parents, are giving birth to little Republicans. What occasionally can result within this counter-swing is a more benign re-arrangement of the present translations; for example, student protests sometimes *are* legitimate protests.

The point is that neither prelaws nor counter-laws seem to be significant sectors of actual social *transformation*—not on the emergent scale we are now discussing. (All sorts of "translative revolutions" are also possible, of course, especially in material modes of production, technological innovations, etc. These, however, do not necessarily involve actual transformations in structures of consciousness.) If actual social transformations do generally come from some sort of presently outlawed sector, the only one left to consider is that of the translaws. It would be helpful, then, if we could specify more precisely the type of seed crystals that might give birth to the eventual transformation, because merely being a translaw, however authentic, does not ensure being the eventual *legitimate* catalyst of a given transformation.

Perhaps we can surmise where we will find the major future catalysts by looking at the structure-stage they will replace. For, in my strongest opinion, before a true collective transpersonal (e.g., psychic) transformation can occur, rational-individual society will first have to reach its full potential and provide the phase-specific truths, values, and substructures for which it is designed and upon which future transformations will depend, such as appropriate technology, a sophisticated medical base, telecommunications as global bonding via global perspectivism, computer interfacing as an extension of mind, and especially a demythologizing of reality, divinity, and consciousness.

It follows that, in my opinion, the first *large-scale* transformative trends will come through those who have already adequately mastered that rational-individuated operative base. For transrational insight comes *through* and then out of the realm of reason, not around it or away from it or against it. They will come from within, these yogis. They might have first flirted with yogic (spiritual, transpersonal, panenhenic) philosophy during their adolescent counter-law phase, but they will have subsequently come to terms with the law itself and therefore will be in a firm position to consciously move beyond it and not merely unconsciously react to it.

Whether esoteric, mystical, nonfundamentalist Christianity will be able to carry out this transformation, or whether it can even survive the prior, necessary demythologizing and dismantling of its exoteric, patriarchal, mythical accouterments, I do not know. (For a superb account of what this new/renewed Christianity would have to look like, see Jacob Needleman's *Lost Christianity*.) But I am fairly convinced that one of the keys to the specific *type* of future transformation lies in *surface structure compatibility,* that is, in a compatibility of the old and new translations, a *bequeathing of legitimacy* (the old and new have to be different enough to constitute an actual transformation, but similar enough to encourage people to jump, as it were). Therefore, the new yogic (shamanic, panenhenic) translations will likely have certain surface structures that are compatible with (and perhaps occasionally direct continuations of) past surface structure symbolizations. For example, the modern phase of rational-individuation, however otherwise different from its mythic-Christian predecessor, retains an emphasis on personhood and individuality, which is clearly Judeo-Christian in origin and nature (God loves and protects individual souls; the individual person is cherished in the eyes of the Lord; God Himself is a big person, so is His Son, etc.).

Because of this general necessity for surface structure compatibility, I do not believe that Eastern religions will serve as large-scale models for Western transformation, however otherwise significant they might have proven to be in terms of being provocateurs. Their influence will be considerable, to be sure, but in a way that is finally translated and assimilated in the new Western panenhenic worldview, and not merely transplanted *en bloc*. Therefore, if the panenhenic transformation is not esoterically Christian, it would not surprise me if a new and specifically Western mysticism arose, although it would be compatible in surface terms with Christian symbology *and* rational technology. (To give a silly example, but one I have already heard elsewhere: yogic meditation is called "a psychotechnology of contemplative love." In the same vein, notice three phenomena whose deep structure is often that of mystical impulse but whose surface structures are such that they could initially have arisen almost nowhere but in America: biofeedback, widespread LSD use, and *A Course in Miracles*. Those are in some ways authentic yogic-saintly endeavors that became very popular because of *surface structure compatibility* with, respectively, American technology, American drug-oriented medicine/culture, and American fundamentalistic-Protestant belief in magic prayer.) My point is simply that the new Western panenhenic consciousness will say all the right things, use all the right symbols, cater to all the old desires, and it will begin to remake the Western world.

3. The three great domains of human development—childish subconsciousness, adolescent self-consciousness, and mature superconsciousness—are each marked by a dominant psychological attitude: passive dependence, active independence, and actively passive surrender (they stand in the relationship thesis, antithesis, synthesis).[101,93] The point of this section is that the first and last attitudes are often confused by scholars, a confusion that results in certain mistaken conclusions on the nature of spiritual community.[102]

Passive dependence is the disposition of the infant-child self-system, simply because it is not yet developed enough to assume responsibility for the relational exchanges of its basic mana-needs (physiological, safety, belongingness). It depends for its very existence on specific relational exchanges with specific partners: mother, father, significant others. Due to its fledgling boundaries, it is especially open to traumatic displacements, splitting, fragmentation, dissociation. These distortions are particularly significant for future development, because (as outlined in chapter 3, "The Distortion of Relational Exchange"), they tend to reproduce themselves on the higher levels of structural organization as the latter emerge and consolidate. Like a grain of sand caught in the early layers of a pearl, each successive layer is crinkled and weakened at a stress point that keeps reproducing itself. Such stress points for the young self-system especially concern its relation to disciplinary or authority figures, since for the most part this actually represents the relation between its own lower and preverbal structures, especially emotional-sexual and aggressive impulses, and its fledgling symbolic-verbal and mental structures, one of whose jobs will be to subdue and transform the emotional-vital components into higher expressions. That is, the interpersonal relation between child and parent is also the intrapersonal relation between the child's own body and mind. Neither relationship can the child yet master, and thus both basically highlight the child's fundamental mood of passive dependence.

All of which changes, or can change, with the emergence in adolescence of the critical, self-reflexive, self-conscious mentality.[54,66,101] The adolescent rebellion against the parents is largely an outward symptom of the inner (and healthy) fight to differentiate from or transcend childish dependence and magic-mythic subconsciousness. The prelaw of the child gives way to the counter-law of the adolescent. There is a corresponding swing in mood from general passive dependence to active independence (again, this *can* go too far, from counter-law to anti-law, but by and large it is nothing but a healthy differentiation and transformation).

The adolescent mood of active independence is a phase-specific form of transcendence—the transcendence from subconscious dependence to self-conscious responsibility.[101] But if it persists beyond its phase-specific moment—which in most Western cultures it does—it acts merely to *prevent* the emergence of the mature disposition of an actively passive surrender of isolated individuality to its own higher and prior nature, or radical superconsciousness, in and as the entire world process at large. This is a *surrender,* in that adolescent swaggering has to be released—died to—in order to make room for rebirth on the superconscient levels. It is *passive,* in that the center of squirming impatience known as ego must eventually relax its chronic contraction in the face of a wider awareness. And it is *actively* passive because it is no mere trancelike submission, but entails an effort of keenest concentration, perception, and will to cut through the obsessive rationalization and stream of contracted thought that constitutes the ego. In the gesture of actively passive surrender, the higher centers of superconscient potential are *actively* engaged, the ego is rendered open and *passive,* and consequently the egoic self-sense can relax into, and *surrender* as, the wider currents of being and awareness that constitute the goal and ground of its own develop-ment—a surrender that marks the end of its own self-alienation.[7,22,45,105]

Now the only reason I bring all this up is that the discipline of actively passive surrender, especially under the guidance of an acknowledged spiritual master, is always being confused with childish passive depen-dence.[93,102] By "always" I mean, specifically, that the vast majority of orthodox psychologists and sociologists do not wish, or are not able, to tell the difference between prepersonal helplessness and dependence on a paternal authority figure, and transpersonal surrender and submission via a spiritual adept. For those scholars, apparently, the adolescent stance of active independence and fierce isolation is held to be, not a phase-specific moment in the greater arc of development, but the goal and highest stage of development itself, whereupon any stance other than that is viewed with ghoulish academic fascination.

Now, it is certainly true that many of the "new religions," or at least the new cults, are based on the dynamics of prepersonal regression/fixa-tion, with consequent obedience to a father figure/totem master, with self-clan fusion and indissociation (participation mystique), with group ritual, magic incantations, mythic apocrypha. The members of the clan-cult often show borderline neurotic or borderline psychotic disposi-tions; that is, low ego-strength, concrete immersion in experience with difficulty holding abstract locations, narcissistic involvement, low self-esteem, with correlative difficulty handling moral ambiguity, contra-dictions, or choice structures.[4,56,59] The clan-cult is magnetic for such personalities, because it (and usually its totem master) offers and fosters an atmosphere of passive dependence to authoritarianism, which re-creates the child-specific mood in which such personalities are still psy-chologically trapped. Cults do not have to "brainwash" such members; all they have to do is show up and smile.

Because it caters to the child-specific mood of passive dependence, the one thing *not* allowed in the clan-cult is the exercise of active adolescent independence, especially the exercise of rational self-reflection, critical appraisal, logical discourse, and systematic study of alternative philoso-phies. This, coupled with the allegiance to totem master, or the magical "father" of the entire clan, constitutes much of the psychosocial founda-tion of the cult.

To the untutored eye, a community of transpersonal contemplatives—what the Buddhists call a *sangha*—often appears similar or even identi-cal to the clan-cult, principally because, I suppose, it is usually rather close-knit and often organized around a spiritual adept held in various degrees of reverence or at least profound respect. This community is also interested in nullifying adolescent active independence, but in an entirely different direction—its transcendence, not its prohibition. In fact, because each higher stage transcends but *includes* its predecessors, the true sangha always *retains access to,* and retains an appropriate place for, rational inquiry, logical reflection, systematic study of other philosophical frameworks, and critical appraisal of its own teachings in light of related areas. Historically, in fact, the mystical centers of contemplation have often been the great centers of education and learning—Nalanda in India, for instance, or the T'ien T'ai Buddhist centers in China. Needham[64] has already demonstrated that mysticism and scientific inquiry have usually been historically linked, simply because both have always rejected dogmatic belief and insisted on open experience.

The point is that what one is attempting to "destroy" in contemplation *is not the mind but an exclusive identity of consciousness with the mind.*[101,102] The infant-child is identified more or less exclusively with the body; as the adolescent mind emerges, it destroys the exclusive identity with the body but does not destroy the body itself; it subsumes the body in its own larger mental identity. Just so, as spirit emerges, it destroys the exclusive identity with mind (and subsumed body) but does not destroy the mind itself; it subsumes the mind to its own larger supreme identity.[102] The mind itself is perfectly valued, as is its free and critical inquiry into any theoretical area.

The adolescent separate-self sense, however, which is an exclusive identification with mind in a stance of rebellious independence, is not so highly valued; therefore, many preliminary exercises in contemplative communities are specifically designed to remind the ego of its phase-specific and intermediate place in overall development. Exercises such as simple bowing in Zen, the prostrations in Vajrayana, or mandatory community service-dharma in monastic sects are outward and visible signs of an inward and actively passive surrender to a state of selfless being more panoramic than ego. The eventual aim of such practices is to keep the mind but transcend the egoic self-sense by discovering a larger self in the spiritual dimension of creation at large.

Now, that is radically different from the clan-cult strategy of *reducing* the self to prepersonal and passive dependence by restricting and prohibiting the free engagement of critical reflection. The aim of sangha is to keep mind but transcend ego; the aim of the cult is to prohibit both.

I realize that in practice it is not always easy to determine whether a particular community is a cult or a sangha—like most life situations, there is something of a continuum between ideal limits. But I feel that the above criteria at least offer a plausible basis for the psychodynamic distinction between these groups (for an expansion of these criteria, see note 106). There is obviously much research to be done in this area, but speaking both personally and as a transpersonal psychologist, I think orthodox psychologists and sociologists could show a little more imagination when it comes to reporting on the psychodynamics of a communal occasion; they have all but made Jonestown a paradigm of "spiritual" get-togethers. I would only like to suggest that an honest effort be made to distinguish child-specific passive dependence from mature actively passive surrender, with a correlative distinction between prepersonal cults and transpersonal sanghas.

4. I have, throughout this book, been emphasizing what sociology might gain from an infusion of psychology (and transpersonal psychology in particular). I should like to emphasize, however, that this is a two-way street, and that psychology (and transpersonal psychology in particular) has much to gain from a study of modern sociology, and especially the sociology of religions. Accordingly, I should like to end this chapter by reprinting my review of *In Gods We Trust: New Patterns of Religious Pluralism in America* (Robbins and Anthony, eds.), which was published in *Journal of Transpersonal Psychology*. That book is representative of the type of serious, disciplined sociological inquiry that is now occurring with regard to various new religious movements in America (though we could almost say, with certain surface modifications, the Western world at large). Other such volumes are, at this moment, being compiled. No question: this is good news—for psychology, sociology, *and* religion.

My comments on this book, while not nearly as detailed as what has gone above, may nonetheless serve as a general summary of our discussion thus far, and as an indication of the type of interdisciplinary dialogue upon which the future of this field depends.

Assuming that psychology is always also social psychology, a study of the "new religions" from a decidedly sociological perspective would be of great significance to psychology in general and to transpersonal psychology/therapy in particular; even more so given the fact that a "transpersonal sociology" is a discipline desperately awaiting birth. *In Gods We Trust* is, I believe, the first rigorously sociological treatment of the new religious movements; as such, it possesses all of the strengths of a truly pioneering effort, and some of the unavoidable weaknesses; in any event, its simple appearance is monumental.

The anthology has as its starting point (and in many ways its central theme) Robert Bellah's immensely influential concept of "civil religion" and its recent disintegration. The idea, briefly, is that, whatever else the function of religion, it serves centrally as a way to meaningfully integrate and legitimate a world view [rd-2 and rd-8]. According to Bellah, American civil religion is (or was) a blend of Biblical symbolism and American nationalism ("One nation, under God. . . ."), a "religion" which adequately served social integration, ethic, and purpose for the better part of American history. However, in recent decades, according to Bellah and others, the American civil religion began to disintegrate, or, technically, to lose its legitimacy (what Bellah calls "the broken covenant"). Assuming (as these theorists do) that religion as integrative function [rd-2] is a universal necessity or impulse, it follows that *something* would have to take the place of the old civil religion; hence, the new religions of the last few decades: "The appeal of oriental mysticism and quasi-mystical therapy groups can best be understood in relation to the needs created by this decline [in civil religion]."

From that point, the anthology moves progressively into various sociological theories, research, and data, arranged in six sections. The subtitles tell the story: Religious Ferment and Cultural Transformation; Disenchantment and Renewal in Mainline Traditions; Civil Religion Sects, Oriental Mysticism and Therapy Groups; The Brainwashing Explanation (since I won't discuss this topic in the rest of this review, let me point out here that this book stands as a sound indictment of the "brainwashing" theory wherever it appears; the data simply doesn't support such an explanatory theory, even with such problematic groups as the Moonies); New Religions; and the Decline of Community. Some highlights:

Robert Wuthnow's "Political Aspects of the Quietistic Revival" is almost humorously titled (re: "quietistic"), because it effectively challenges the longstanding prejudice (found in researchers from Weber to Freud) that there is a " 'hydraulic relation' between experiential religion and political commitment, that the more mystical a person is, the less involved in [social or] political activity he is likely to be." On the basis of empirical data, Wuthnow demonstrates that not only are those attracted to mysticism *not* less socially committed, they consistently ranked higher in most social commitment categories (e.g., value of social improvement, equal rights for women, solving social problems, etc.). Related is Donald Stone's "Social Consciousness in the Human Potential Movement." Based on systematically collected data, Stone suggests that at least some (not all) of the human potential movements tend to increase social responsibility by *lessening,* not increasing, narcissistic withdrawal, *contra* Lasch and other critics (although this by no means invalidates all of Lasch's arguments, which apparently do apply to some "new age" movements, the differential remaining unspecified [a differential I have suggested as prelaw versus translaw]).

Robert Bellah's chapter is a clarification of his concept of "civil religion," as well as a cogent argument that, in effect, the American constitution implicitly but fatally assumed moral discipline (or purpose) would always be effected by the Church, so that, as the Church now declines, there is no obvious national moral replacement; some of the new religions then offer, not a legitimate replacement for fractured moral bonding, but a privatistic escape ("so self-centered that they begin to approximate the consumer cafeteria model").

Robbins and Anthony's own contribution includes a superb introduction—perhaps the best single chapter in the anthology; a complete and devastating critique of the brainwashing model; and an insightful report on the Meher Baba community. The latter is especially important, because it demonstrates that sophisticated sociological analysis (largely Parsonian) can be performed on a spiritual community without reductionistically denigrating the community or its teachings. (In so doing, it everywhere transcends, however subtly, strict Parsonianism.)

Finally, as a general statement, the empirical sociological data presented in the volume is both interesting and significant, demonstrating the considerable power of sociological methodology.

Because psychologists tend to study trees and not forests, and because sociologists tend to study forests and not trees, these disciplines seem always to need balancing via interdisciplinary dialogue. This seems especially true for the psychology and sociology of religion. For instance, a transpersonal psychologist might wish to point out that a few of the book's chapters contain subtle reductionistic tendencies. For example, if the "new religions" are basically the result of the disintegration of American civil religion, is that *all* they are? Is what Zen Buddhism offers *essentially* the same as what civil religion offered? Many sociologists say yes; a transpersonal psychologist would probably say no. The latter religion offered an integration of egos, the former, their transcendence—a fact that sociology as sociology tends to miss. (Although I must mention that the editors of this volume are, in their own writings, acutely attuned to this distinction.) A transpersonal psychologist might therefore acknowledge the sociological perspective by saying that the breakdown of the old civil religion was necessary but *not sufficient* for the recent interest in authentic mystical religions. *Necessary,* in that if there were no disharmony at all in orthodox religions, one would not seek elsewhere; *not sufficient,* in that the new authentically mystical traditions offer something *never* officially offered by civil or orthodox religions: actual transcendence (and not merely communal immersion).

For the same reasons, a transpersonal psychologist might point out that there seems to be a stark difference between *transpersonal* growth and *prepersonal* regression; that some of the so-called new religions or new therapies are actually prepersonal, not transpersonal; that these prepersonal movements are indeed often narcissistic, cultic, authoritarian, anti-rational, and self-centered (although via the "group self" [i.e., mythic-membership]); and these cultic movements—Jonestown, Synanon, Children of God—cannot believably be equated with authentic transpersonal sanghas, or contemplative communities—such as, perhaps, various genuine Buddhist centers (Zen, Vajrayana, Theravada), Christian mystical enclaves, some Yoga centers, etc. But again, sociology *as* sociology [or functionalism bereft of hierarchic structuralism] tends to miss these types of distinctions, since it sees only what these forests have in common: they are all different from mainstream, orthodox religions.

But if those are the types of things sociology might learn from transpersonal psychology, *In Gods We Trust* is an extraordinary compendium of what transpersonal psychologists can learn from modern sociology. I mean explicitly to include psychologists in general, but transpersonal psychologists and therapists in particular. For, as we said, if such theories are not sufficient for transpersonalists, they nevertheless remain absolutely necessary. Just as psychoanalysis of productions "on the couch" can't tell you about the sanity of society at large, so the study of the productions "on the zazen mat" can't tell you about larger and equally significant societal currents. In my opinion, many of the recalcitrant theoretical problems faced by transpersonal psychology have already been substantially answered by the sociology of religion, and *In Gods We Trust* is exactly a compendium of such answers.

This anthology is all the more significant given the commitment of its editors. Dick Anthony, for instance, is acutely aware of the difference between regressive, prepersonal, and prerational movements and progressive, transpersonal, and transrational concerns. His work is permeated with a genuine sensitivity to nonreductionistic interpretations of spiritual endeavors. Moreover, he is, in conjunction with Jacob Needleman, Thomas Robbins, and others, almost singlehandedly initiating the dialogue between orthodox sociologists and transpersonal psychologists. *In Gods We Trust* is not that dialogue—it is (and was appropriately intended to be) a genuinely sociological anthology, with little psychology, transpersonal or otherwise. But beyond that stated aim, which it thoroughly achieves, it is an invitation to a future dialogue with transpersonal psychologists, an invitation whose significance cannot be overestimated, and an invitation to which I trust psychologists in general, and transpersonal psychologists in particular, will enthusiastically respond.

8

Knowledge and Human Interests

I N THIS CHAPTER I would like to take Habermas's work on knowledge and cognitive interests as a starting base for extending sociology, and especially a critical sociology, into a more truly comprehensive formulation, one capable of adequately embracing authentically spiritual or actually transcendental *knowledge* and *interest*. Since I wish only to suggest certain possibilities, the discussion will be conducted on a more than usually generalized and preliminary level.

Habermas[38] distinguishes three principal modes of knowledge-inquiry: the empirical-analytic, which deals with objectifiable processes; the historical-hermeneutic, which aims at interpretive understanding of symbolic configurations; and the critical-reflective, which apprehends (past) cognitive operations and thus subjects them to a measure of insight.

The especially intriguing part of Habermas's theory is that each mode is intrinsically linked to a type of human *interest,* for knowledge as knowledge is always moved and moving. To get an idea of what Habermas means by cognitive interests, if every time you wanted to know something you asked yourself, "*Why* do I want to know this?" and then removed all the purely personal-idiosyncratic motives, you would have the *general cognitive interest* that guides the particular process of inquiry.

According to Habermas,[38] "The approach of the empirical-analytic sciences incorporates a *technical* cognitive interest; that of the historic-hermeneutic sciences incorporates a *practical* one; and the approach of critically oriented sciences incorporates the *emancipatory* cognitive interest." *Technical* interest is interest in predicting and controlling events in the objectifiable environment. *Practical* interest is interest in understanding and sharing the mutualities of life, morality, purpose, goals, values, and such. *Emancipatory* interest is interest in releasing the distortions and constraints of labor, language, or communication that result from their nontransparency, or their not being looked at steadily with critical awareness. (At this point, I remind the reader that we have earlier distinguished between horizontal emancipation, which aims at redressing the distortions within any given level, and vertical emancipation, which aims at moving to a higher level altogether. Habermas treats only the former, and therefore I will always refer to his as horizontal-emancipatory interest.)

I am now going to take two shortcuts. First, I am going to use only our three general domains of the sub, self, and superconscient, by the names of physical-sensorimotor, mental-rational, and spiritual-transcendental, or body, mind, and spirit for short. Body possesses a degree of *pre*-symbolic or sensory knowledge; mind works with symbolic knowledge; and spirit deals with *trans*-symbolic knowledge or gnosis. Notice that mind, being *the* symbolic mode, can form symbols *of* each of the three domains: the material world, the mental world itself, and the spiritual world. Those three modes of symbolic knowledge, when added to transsymbolic gnosis and presymbolic awareness, give us five general modes of cognition. Figure 4 indicates these modes.

Number 1 is spiritual gnosis, or spirit's direct and nonmediated knowledge *of* spirit *as* spirit. Number 2a is what has been called paradoxical or mandalic reason, because it is mind's attempt to put into

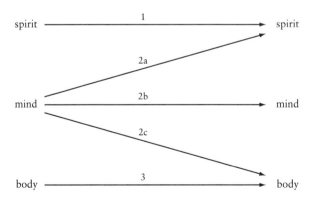

FIGURE 4. Five General Modes of Cognition.

mental symbols that which is finally transmental, and the result is always eventually paradoxical. Number 2b is mind's knowledge of other minds, or a symbol's awareness of other symbols, as when you are reading this. Number 2c is the mind's awareness of the physical and sensory world, or the symbol-models used to picture the *pre*-symbolic world. Number 3 is the sensorimotor apprehension of the sensorimotor world, or the presymbolic grasp of the presymbolic world.*

In my opinion, those forms of knowledge are *grounded* in the levels of *structural organization* themselves. The deep structures of developmental or self-forming consciousness dictate the very *forms* of those cognitions; to that extent they are largely invariant, deep-rooted, native, and collective (although, of course, their surface structures are in large measure culturally molded and conditioned).

My second shortcut is to identify Habermas's empirical-analytic mode with number 2c, or mind's awareness of the empirical-sensory world; and his historical-hermeneutic mode with number 2b, or mind's interaction with other minds. This is a shortcut because the distinctions are not precise; for example, insofar as a hermeneutic occasion has an empirically objective component, that component can become object to empirical-analytic inquiry; likewise, insofar as a sensory-objective occasion comes under interpretive understanding, it can become object to historical-hermeneutic inquiry. Nonetheless, it is my opinion that the central form, the very paradigm, of empirical-analytic inquiry is symbolic mind reflecting presymbolic world, and the paradigm of historical-hermeneutic inquiry is symbolic mind interacting with symbolic mind. To put it crudely, the former is mind reflecting matter; the latter, mind reflecting mind. As a generalization, then, we use number 2b as historical-hermeneutic and number 2c as empirical-analytic, and we assign them their respective cognitive interests, practical-moral and technical-predictive, which are all listed in figure 5 (page 118).

What, then, are we to make of Habermas's horizontal-emancipatory interest, the interest in "clearing up" the distortions in relational exchange on each major level? If knowledge and human interests are really grounded in *structures,* we should be able to point to a central structure as paradigmatic for this emancipatory interest (as we pointed to number 2c for empirical-technical, etc.). And yet, for reasons that will become clearer as we proceed, none of the five cognitive modes quite fits the bill. For one thing, horizontal-emancipatory interest apparently can operate

* See *Eye to Eye* for a fuller discussion of these modes.

on all or almost all levels. For another, it is not *necessarily* operative, but comes into existence only if there have, in fact, been distortions that demand clarification. As Habermas[38] puts it:

> Compared with the technical and practical interests in knowledge, which are both grounded in deeply rooted (invariant? [i.e., deep?]) structures of action and experience . . . , the [horizontal-] *emancipatory interest in knowledge* has a derivative status. It guarantees the connection between theoretical knowledge and an "object domain" of practical life which comes into existence as a result of systematically distorted communication and thinly legitimated repression.

The horizontal-emancipatory interest, in other words, is rooted not so much in specific structures per se, for it then would be continually active, but rather in structural *tension* caused by structural distortion, and its aim is to remove the source of the tension. Once the distortions are gone, the horizontal-emancipatory interest loses its juice. It is therefore not surprising that the only two major instances of such horizontal-emancipatory concerns given by Habermas (other than his own work) are Freudian psychoanalysis and Marxist materialist critique.

To put it simplistically, the need for psychoanalysis arises only when something "goes wrong" in psychological development. Psychological distortions—repressions and oppressions—give rise to psychological tensions; these tensions can be resolved only by a critical reflection on, or analysis of, "what went wrong" itself, and this critical-reflective knowledge has as its *interest* the *emancipation* from those distortions, obstructions, and repressions. Marxist material-economic critique operates in a similar fashion—past (historical) economic oppressions give rise to societal tensions. These tensions (class struggle, false consciousness, alienated labor, opaque ideology) can be resolved only by a critical analysis of their historical (development) genesis, with an interest in the emancipation from such oppressive economic distortions. And what Habermas himself is doing, with his philosophy of communicative ethics, is using critical-reflective inquiry and horizontal-emancipatory interest in an attempt to illumine and then correct the distortions and restraints placed upon what should otherwise be free and open *communicative exchange*. The oppression of communication and intersubjective exchange gives rise to distortions in discourse (and truth) itself—propaganda being the simplest example. Such "systematically distorted communication and thinly legitimated repression" generates both the possibility and the necessity for critical-reflective inquiry into such distortions with an interest in the emancipation from such opaque communication. *In all three cases,* once the distortions are cleared, the need for analysis and the interest in emancipation both tend to wane, since they have served their purpose by dissolving their own source.

I would simply add that, in my opinion, the fact that Freud and Marx were both aware of the importance of communicative exchange in their various fields should not conceal the fact that material-economic obstruction (which most but not solely interested Marx), emotional-sexual obstruction (which most but not solely interested Freud), and communicative obstruction (which most but not solely interests Habermas) refer to quite different structural levels of relational exchange and potential distortion. *The horizontal-emancipatory interest can swing into play with regard to each,* but the actual dynamics are slightly different in each case because the object domain of each has a different structure. To put it simply, "clearing up" matter, clearing up sex, and clearing up communication are all forms of horizontal-emancipation, but the concrete dynamics differ in each case because the dynamics of matter, emotions, and thoughts are themselves different. After all, the murder of Socrates, for example, was not a result of economic-material distortion nor emotional-sexual repression, but communicative oppression. These various distortions, like the levels they infect, are hierarchic. And in that hierarchy of disease, what Marx did *primarily* for the material sphere, and Freud did *primarily* for the emotional sphere, Habermas is now doing primarily for the communicative (mental) sphere. Those three theorists stand as exemplars of the horizontal-emancipatory interest on those levels. (We are still awaiting the analyst who as brilliantly studies the distortions and oppressions of spirituality, the repression of transcendence, the politics of Tao, the denial of Being by beings.)

We can now fill out figure 5 by adding the other forms of knowledge and their respective interests. I tentatively suggest the following: the interest of mode number 3, or bodily knowledge of the sensory world, is *instinctual*; the schemata of sensorimotor cognition are grounded in instinctual survival. The interest of mode number 2a, or the mind's attempt to reason about spirit, is *soteriological*—interest in salvation; an attempt to comprehend spirit in mental terms so as either to orient oneself toward the pull of a transcendental intuition or to help "picture" the spiritual realm for those minds not yet so *interested*. (The picture is always eventually paradoxical, as both Kant and Nagarjuna explained, but this neither hampers the human interest in the divine nor restricts the usefulness of mandalic reason; e.g., there is some sort of useful information carried in the paradoxical-mandalic statement that spirit is both perfectly transcendent and perfectly immanent.) The interest of gnosis, mode number 1, or spirit's knowledge of spirit as spirit, is *liberational*—interest in radical liberation (satori, moksha, wu, release). Where soteriological interest wishes to present to the self a higher knowledge, liberational interest aims at dissolving the self into higher knowledge *as* that knowledge, that is, as spirit's knowledge of and as spirit. The former wishes, as self, to be saved by spirit; the latter wishes, as spirit, to transcend self.

It remains to comment on the vertical-emancipatory interest. Like its cousin the horizontal-emancipatory interest, it is generated not so much by a specific structure as by a structural *tension,* and its interest is to remove the source of the tension. But here the source is not a tension *within* a particular level but a tension *between* levels; specifically, the tension of *emergence,* the tension of a coming transformation, or vertical shift in levels of structural organization. The aim of this vertical-emancipatory interest is to free awareness, not from a distortion that might or might not happen within a level, but from the relatively limited perspective offered by that level even at its best—and to do so by opening awareness to the next higher level of structural organization. This interest cannot be allayed by clearing up the distortions within a level but only by the emergence of the next higher level. We may suppose that the interest then temporarily wanes, until (and if) the inherent limitations of the next level begin increasingly to display themselves, and emancipation *from,* not *within,* that level increasingly exerts itself. Barring arrest, such vertical-emancipatory interest will continue periodically until final emancipation, that is, until satori. At that point, the last form of vertical-emancipatory interest coincides precisely with liberational interest; that is, the two are the same at the asymptotic limit of growth. All in all, the interest of horizontal-emancipation is to clear up translation; the interest of vertical-emancipation is to promote transformation.

Figure 5 lists all of these modes of knowledge and their interests.

My point, then, introductory as it may be, is that when we add these various modes and interests of human knowledge to the various levels of structural organization and relational exchange of the human compound individual, with all the corollaries and psychosocial displays suggested in the other chapters, we have the outlines of a fairly comprehensive (though far from completed) cultural theory: a skeleton, as it were. We have most of the bones here, even if we do not know yet

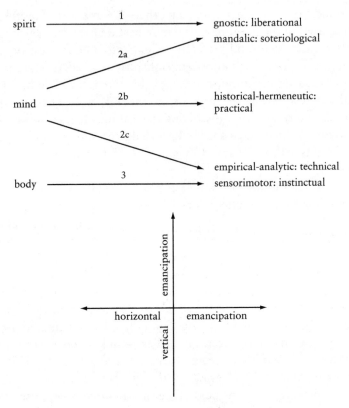

FIGURE 5. Modes of Knowledge and Their Interests.

everything to hang on them. But at least we make perfect and appropriate room for the prepersonal, the personal, and the transpersonal dimensions of existence—their levels, their development, their social exchange nature, their possible repressive (psychological) and oppressive (social) distortions, their modes of knowing and interest, their structural organization, their functional relations. And it is a truly *critical* and *normative* sociological theory, by virtue of the two emancipatory interests that rear their heads wherever structural nonfreedom and nontransparency arise. This critical (what went wrong) and normative (what should go right) dimension, especially in its vertical form, is not based *on* ideological preference, dogmatic inclination, or theoretical conjecture, but *in* the observable, verifiable, inherently preferred direction of structural development and evolution, a direction that discloses itself in successive hierarchic emancipations that *themselves* pass judgments on their less transcendental predecessors.

9

Methodology, Summary, and Conclusion

I WOULD LIKE TO summarize and conclude this outline by giving an example of proposed methodology in a sociological investigation of a religious group, with specific emphasis on any psychotherapeutic counseling that might be requested (not that such therapy is necessary, but the topic always seems to come up with regard to "religious groups," and so I will take the opportunity to comment in general). This will be merely a specialized example of the overall sociological methodology implicit in the model we have presented throughout this book.

STRUCTURAL ANALYSIS (DETERMINATION OF AUTHENTICITY)

1. Whenever sociologists are met with an apparently religious expression, they may, in addition to other methodological approaches (described below), perform a *structural* analysis on the *form* of the expressions, symbologies, psychosocial exchanges, and so forth. The aim of such standard structural analysis is, by means of increasingly subtracting/abstracting the surface structures, to arrive at the deep structure underlying and governing the operations (i.e., translations) of the surface structures themselves.[5,70,101] This analysis aims, in effect, to assign all surface structures to their appropriate deep structure by demon-

strating that they obey the transcriptive rules of the particular deep structure (or that they can, via transcription, be resolved into the deep structure).

Such structural analyses might include any of the tests devised by, for example, Kohlberg; Loevinger; Broughton; Sullivan, Grant, and Grant; Isaacs; Peck; Bull; Selman; and Graves. That these various formulations are all *roughly* correlative has been demonstrated by Loevinger;[57] in any event, they suffice perfectly to give us a first approximation of the degree of general structural organization reached by the central belief systems embraced by the group. We are not so much interested in the scores of any *particular* members, although those can certainly be ascertained (and should be ascertained for any member specifically seeking counseling). Rather, we wish structurally to analyze the central belief systems by which the group *defines itself.* One way of determining this is to structurally analyze the occasion that *defines membership in the group*; that is, What interaction, series of interactions, or belief structures must be internalized by a person in order to be socially *recognized* as a member of this group? What has to be "in" a person before the person is officially "in" the group? What level of "food" has to be digested by initiates in order to be "family"? For it is *that* occasion, embodying *that* mana, which marks the central-level or base-level of structural organization by which the group defines its self-identity and around which the group as group inevitably revolves. If there are levels of initiation/belief, analysis is applied at each level. (As for structural tests for the higher-authentic levels, see below, item 3 on page 121)

2. Once an approximate determination of central-level deep structure has been made, its relative location on the developmental hierarchy of structuralization can be determined. For example, is this "religious involvement" archaic, magical, mythical, rational, centauric, psychic, subtle, causal, nondual? (Or, for example, Loevinger: symbiotic, impulsive, self-protective, conformist, conscientious, individualistic, autonomous, integrated? and so on.)

This determination—or something like it—is especially important for counseling purposes, because in psychotherapeutic service (and social work) it is a great advantage, as psychoanalytic ego psychology has clearly demonstrated, to know the degree of structuralization reached by the self-system in question.[17] Are there archaic fusion elements (self-group indissociation, archaic-uroboric "oneness," oral-cannibalistic trends)? Is there borderline structure present (magical-psychotic, animistic, totem confusion, delusional reference systems)? Is there extreme mythic-membership conformity (with terror of individuality, surrender of self-will and determination, yearning for belongingness and cultic association, passive dependence on authority figures)? Is there rational structure but with possible complicating side-issues (merely and more or less healthy counter-law tendencies, or actual neurotic splitting, symptomology, and identity crisis)? Is there actual psychic, subtle, or causal structure, but with consequent alienation from mainstream mythic or rational consensus (communication viscosity, social isolation, possible depression)?

I cannot emphasize too strongly the importance of such structural diagnosis; without it, any therapeutic intervention can be disastrous.[102] As only a simple example, take the differences between prerational and transrational engagements. A prerational, borderline individual, who needs desperately to create rational structure and ego strength, should not be introduced to the more strenuous transrational meditative-yogic disciplines, because they are designed to *loosen* the rational structure temporarily and thus will simply dismantle what little structure the borderline has left. Likewise, such clients, in my opinion, should not be exposed to "experiential" therapies, since they already live too much in the experience and not enough in the mind.[17] Conversely, someone beginning or undergoing a true transformation to psychic-subtle realms will find no help from an orthodox psychiatrist, who tends to see all transrational development as prerational regression, and who, in helping to re-entrench exclusive rational structure in this person, will deliver his or her spiritual consciousness stillborn. Such a person should be referred to a qualified spiritual master, Jungian therapist, transpersonal psychologist, or some other authentically oriented service.

In short, the aim of structural analysis is to determine the *type,* and consequently the *degree,* of developmental structuralization and organization, and correlatively, if the situation claims religiosity, its degree of authenticity.

3. The above analysis, of course, will eventually hinge on a more refined developmental-structural hierarchy than we have presented here. The refinement and sophistication of this hierarchy will occur through the continued structural-developmental-stage research in psychological cognition, identity, perception, normalization, natural epistemology, and so on. This refinement is already occurring—has been occurring for quite some time—on the subconscient and self-conscient realms of structuralization, under the names of psychoanalytic developmental psychology, cognitive psychology, genetic epistemology, developmental ego psychology, and so on. As interest and research increasingly extend to

the superconscient realms, we will naturally (I assume) witness a re-finement-sophistication of the developmental-structural hierarchies with regard to the higher and contemplative levels. The initial phases of this research seem likely to follow two stages.

a. *Hermeneutical reading of authentic texts:* In order to map out re-search design and strategy, it is necessary to have some sort of working hypotheses, and one of the best sources of such working sets seems to be the experimental-maps of superconscious stages offered by the tradi-tional texts. A careful and systematic hermeneutical reading of the vari-ous (esoteric) religious texts will help provide us with a fund of working hypotheses-maps around which to frame actual research and against which to judge initial progress. *The Atman Project* is a basic but very general attempt in this direction, drawing on *cross-cultural parallels* to suggest some basic deep structures of the higher stage-levels (centauric, low-subtle, high-subtle, low-causal, high-causal, and ultimate, which I have condensed in this book to psychic, subtle, causal, and ultimate). Daniel Brown[20] has presented a hermeneutical reading of one particular stage-conception of higher meditative states, that of Mahamudra, which is the type of detailed hermeneutics we will need in each esoteric tradi-tion so that we can draw more precisely our cross-cultural parallels and conclusions. The works of Pascal Kaplan,[55] Daniel Goleman,[35] Huston Smith,[86] Fritjof Schuon,[81] and René Guénon[37] are important guides in this endeavor.

b. *Direct investigation:* In order to test our refined hypothetical maps, we will need actual data accumulation from populations of those genu-inely engaged in superconscient development and adaptation. This topic itself demands no less than book-length treatment, and instead of even trying to mention all the pertinent points (and problems), I will only say that, using the hermeneutical working maps, we will be able to design proposed characterologies of the higher structure-stages, construct ade-quate tests to register and measure the emergence and degree of these traits, and eventually subject the results to standard structural analyses à la Piaget, Kohlberg, Loevinger, and others. These will be repeated wherever possible in cross-cultural conditions (Japan, India, Burma, etc., have very large contemplative sectors, as does now the United States). Initial work is being done in this area by Maliszewski, Twemlow, Brown, Engler, Gabbard, Jones, and others.[21,58,92]

I feel this field is especially ripe for sociologists, since almost all re-search to date has overlooked the intersubjective patterns of relational exchange that constitute the higher as well as lower levels of structural adaptation. Psychologists interested only in perceptual changes, cognitive shifts, affect reinterpretation, or impulse control of meditators tend to overlook the psycho*social* nature of their artificially isolated data, just as psychoanalysts tended to overlook the fact that analysis of productions "on the couch" cannot tell you that the society at large might itself be sick, and adaptation to a sick society is a poor criterion of "mental health." Just as analysis of social patterns at large cannot be conducted on the couch, so identification of the fundamental psychosocial relationships constitutive of the contemplative realms cannot be conducted on the zazen mat. Transpersonal psychology will eventually have to find itself in transpersonal sociology.

As for the direct investigation of the superconscient realms, as opposed to indirect psychological or sociological data accumulation, see below, "The Methodology of Direct Gnostic Verification" (page 128).

FUNCTIONAL ANALYSIS (DETERMINATION OF LEGITIMACY)

1. Once the degree of authenticity of the religious expression is determined via structural analysis, the degree of legitimacy can be determined via standard functionalist (systems theory) approaches. The point is simply to determine how well the particular religious engagement is serving stability and integration *within* the group itself (content legitimacy) and *between* the group and its broader societal background (context legitimacy). Here all the standard functional analyses and more or less empirical-analytic determinations swing into play—tension management, pattern maintenance, boundary determinations, content and context analyses, latent and manifest functions, and so forth[62,69]—but with a refined understanding as to hierarchic levels of structural interaction. For example, if the particular group is determined (via previous structural analysis) to be prelaw, that fact will set a boundary with relation to law that is not merely between two systems but between two different levels of systems, a fact that functionalism itself cannot detect (lacking normative hierarchy). We have to use developmental structuralism to impose this boundary condition, or else the functional analyses tend to slide over (and then collapse into) each other.

With regard to legitimacy/illegitimacy, here are what seem to be some common content and context patterns. Frequently, prelaw sectors (or individuals) are found to be both content *and* context illegitimate, which means that their symbologies and relational exchanges provide little or no internal mana/integration and little or no larger societal co-existence (in which case they are always on the verge of anti-law engagement). However, it is not uncommon to find content and context legitimate prelaw sectors (e.g., stereotypical gypsies, although in America they are supposedly always on the verge of context illegitimacy, i.e., anti-law) or "part-time" prelaw sectors (i.e., serve societal law-translations "by day" and benign but ritual prelaw celebrations "by night," e.g., witches' covens). Perhaps most common, however, are prelaw groups that no matter how possibly content legitimate are context illegitimate (i.e., anti-law; e.g., Hell's Angels).

At the other end of the spectrum, it is not uncommon to find an *authentic* religious expression that is having context legitimation difficulties *because* it is trans-law. Such translaws, therefore, for functional pattern maintenance and tension management, tend to form microcommunities of like-minded practitioners (sanghas), which is simply another way of saying that, since each level of structural adaptation *is* a level of relational exchange, communities of exchange partners are inevitable, and it is within that community that one measure of legitimation is sought (content legitimation). But also we want to watch the boundary phenomena *between* translaw groups and the law-society at large (context legitimation), and, for particular individuals, how they handle (integrate) the structural tensions of living in both sectors.

2. All in all, then, the overall patterns of social interrelation seem to be determined in part by (a) the degree of authenticity and (b) the degree of legitimacy, evidenced (c) within and (d) across each boundary situation. Thus, the *internal content* of a given group will be among the set: (prelaw, counter-law, law, anti-law, translaw) × (legitimate, illegitimate). Likewise, *between* each group and its larger societal background (context) there are the same ten possibilities (although one of them—anti-law context legitimacy—is for all practical purposes an impossibility). The overall result is a display of twenty (or nineteen) different possible cells into which any psychosocial exchange in general, and any religious expression in particular, will fall.

Now by no means am I implying that that analysis is complete or even adequate, and I certainly do not wish to exclude other typologies. My only point is that by adding a basic structural-hierarchical analysis to the standard functional ones, we achieve a vertical (authenticity) scale in addition to a horizontal (legitimacy) scale, and it is this combination that gives us four compass points by which to navigate our sociological investigations.

THE HERMENEUTICAL MOMENT

1. If the structural and functional analyses form the methodological backbone of this approach, they by no means exhaust the necessary approaches. Deep structural analysis *cannot* determine specific surface structure contents and values, just as the rules of chess cannot tell you which moves a particular player will actually make. Nor is overall functionalism helpful here, because it sees forests and not trees. So, for specific understandings of specific individual values, meanings, and expressions, we always rely on phenomenological-hermeneutics. In this task we are helped by our prior structural and functional analyses, for they provide, respectively, the proper narrative foil (i.e., developmental hierarchy) and proper narrative context (i.e., the relation of the individual text to society at large). But in the last analysis, we are face to face with a living person who reads us while we read him or her, and this co-production is a human sharing in which both sides are correspondingly enriched or diminished.

For this general phenomenological-hermeneutics, we have the important works of, for example, Gadamer, Schutz, Berger and Luckmann, Garfinkle, Taylor, Ricoeur.

2. For specific therapeutic service, the hermeneutic procedure involves a conscious *interpretation* of symptoms deemed problematic by the client, with the eventual aim of re-constructing the possible developmental miscarriages that splintered or fragmented the ongoing sweep of structuralization. When this fragmentation occurs, aspects of consciousness are split off and thus become opaque in their meaning. They are "hidden texts," alienated facets of self, dissociated *symbols* that show up as *symptoms*. By *interpreting* the symbol-symptoms—the hidden texts and subtexts—the therapist helps the client to re-own those facets of self by *re-authoring* them and thus re-authorizing them, that is, consciously assuming responsibility for their existence.[105]

This is where a general knowledge of development as ongoing hierarchical structuralization is so essential, because the historical-hermeneutic procedure is not merely digging into past developments on the present level, but into past and *less structured* levels, whose meanings are very difficult to *translate* without a knowledge of past *transformations*. The therapist, for instance, might find that, within the client's rational, linguistic, conscious communication of a particular message or series of messages, there is a hidden meaning, a subtext. Now this opaque subtext might indeed be a fairly rational message itself, but one the client wishes not to acknowledge (taboo for the moment); therapy here involves not much more than the therapist's providing a *context* for the acknowledgment of the rational subtext. However, on occasion the hidden message, the opaque communication, the subtext, is written in *mythic* syntax, which itself might have a core of *magical* wish-fulfillments (which *in turn* are often informed or subtexted by archaic *instinctual* or emotional-sexual interests).[35,101,105]

In such cases, apparently, at some point in the course of early development, a magical (and/or emotional) subtext was deemed taboo and defensively split off (repressed, dissociated) from the ongoing march of structuralization. Since structures are always structures *of* relational exchange, this also involves a *privatization* of what otherwise could form a unit in intersubjective exchange. That is, the alienation from self *is* an alienation from others. Once cut off from personal understanding and removed likewise from all possibility of consensual interpretation, it becomes an illegitimate subtext isolated from the narrative of ongoing development. Thus alienated from immediate narration, isolated and privatized, it tends to draw around itself any other subsequently outlawed elements. Thus gathering layer after layer of *mistranslation* (distorted relational exchange), it finally protrudes into awareness as a baffling symptom. And baffling it is, because, as a doubly secret text, hidden to both self and others, it has no referent for interpretation; it remains clothed in opaque symbols and nontransparent urges. Ask the client why he or she is producing such symptoms or what they mean, and the client replies, "I have no idea; that's why I'm here. Why is this happening? Why won't it stop?" The very fact that the client usually refers to a symptom as "it," instead of "I" or "me" (e.g., "*I* move my hand, but the symptom, *it* happens against my will") mirrors exactly the dissociated, alienated, and foreign state into which the now hidden impulse or subtext or shadow-message has fallen. Indeed, when Freud summarized the goal of therapy as "Where it was, there I shall become" (poorly translated as "Where it was, there ego shall be"), he must have had essentially this crucial point in mind.

Part of the therapeutic procedure, therefore, is to use this knowledge of structural development (archaic to magic to mythic to rational) as a narrative foil against which to interpret the hidden meanings of the various subtexts, until those meanings once again become transparent to the client (i.e., nonrepressed). At that point, the symptom tends to wane because its symbolic content has been released from its privatized alienation to rejoin the community of relational exchange, and its bioenergetic component (should it have one) is released for bodily participation in emotional-sexual sharing, and its overall meaning-message has rejoined the individual's ongoing narrative unfoldment. In this overall procedure, developmental structuralism gives us the external narrative foil, and hermeneutics gives us the various internal-personal meanings of the various subtexts as they unfold against (and because of) the narrative foil itself.

3. There is, as we mentioned earlier, the role of hermeneutics in suggesting initial working maps of the higher realms (via textual analysis of the world's esoteric traditions). Here I would only like to issue a caveat: as researchers such as Daniel Brown have suggested, a hermeneutic reading of esoteric texts discloses hierarchic stages of contemplative development. It is important to remember, however, that the hierarchy or stage-conception itself is *not* a hermeneutical disclosure. The stages are disclosed via developmental-logic—the narrative foil—in actual practice and evolution. These successive *emergent* occasions everywhere surprise narrative; however, when the overall results are simply entered in a text, it may deceptively appear that they are created by the text and therefore discoverable solely by hermeneutics, which is not the whole case, as I tried to suggest in chapter 1, "Phenomenological-Hermeneutics."

EMANCIPATORY MOMENTS

Without belaboring the point, I will take it as obvious that overall therapy involves a critical self-reflection on past translations and possible mistranslations (hidden texts). I believe this is true for individuals as well as for societies at large (although obviously the specifics vary). Such reflection is driven by the *horizontal-emancipatory interest*—a desire to "clear up" past mistranslations (hidden subtexts, repressions, oppressions, dissociations). These distortions, secretly lodged in the hierarchy of the compound individual, generate structural tensions and irritations that drive the emancipatory interest. When such fixations/repressions are re-membered, re-authored, and re-integrated, then those aspects of individual consciousness (or groups of people) formerly trapped in a lower level of structuralization become liberated, or capable of transformation-upward, thus surrendering their symptomatic complaints and rejoining the average higher mode of structuralization now characteristic of the central self (or society at large). Such transformative advance is driven by the *vertical-emancipatory interest* inherent in development and evolution itself.

THE METHODOLOGY OF DIRECT GNOSTIC VERIFICATION

There is, finally, the methodological problem of the *direct* (as opposed to textual) investigation of the higher (superconscient) levels themselves, and here we draw on our last two major modes of inquiry: gnosis/jnana for direct apprehension of these levels, and mandalic-logic to communicate them, however paradoxically, in linguistic symbols. For spiritual knowledge itself is *not* symbolic; it involves direct, nonmediated, transsymbolic intuition of and identity with spirit.[7,22,88] As I have tried to suggest elsewhere,[99] this spiritual knowledge, *like all other forms of valid cognitive knowledge,* is experimental, repeatable, and publicly verifiable, because, like all other valid modes, it consists of three strands:

1. *Injunction:* always of the form, "If you want to know this, *do* this."
2. *Apprehension:* a cognitive apprehension-illumination of the "object domain" addressed by the injunction.
3. *Communal confirmation:* a checking of results with others who have adequately completed the injunctive and illuminative strands.

I shall give an example of all three strands in, say, empirical-analytic sciences. If you want to know whether a cell really contains a nucleus, then you must (1) learn to operate a microscope, learn to take histological sections, learn to stain cells, and so forth (injunctions), then (2) look and see (apprehension), then (3) compare your apprehensions with those of others, especially a qualified teacher if you are just beginning, or a community of like-minded scientific adepts if you are professionally continuing a career (communal confirmation).

Bad injunctive theories (no. 1) will be rebuffed by noncongruent apprehensions (no. 2) and subsequently rejected by the community of investigators (no. 3), and it is this potential rebuff that constitutes the nonverifiability principle of Popper.

Just so with authentic spiritual knowledge. For example, we will take Zen, vis-à-vis the three strands. It has an injunctive strand, which requires years of specialized training and critical discipline: the practice of meditation, or zazen, which is the injunctive tool for possible cognitive disclosure. Not surprisingly, then, it is always of the form "If you want to know whether there is Buddha-nature, you must first do this." That is *experimental* and *experiential* injunction.

After that strand is mastered, the investigator is opened to the second strand, that of apprehension-illumination; in this case, satori. Satori is a "direct seeing into one's nature"—as perfectly direct as looking into the microscope to see the cell nucleus, with the important proviso in each case: only a trained eye need look.

The third strand is careful confirmation, by both a Zen Master and the community of participant meditators. This is no merely automatic pat on the back and mutual-agreement society; it is a vigorous *test,* and it constitutes a potentially powerful rebuff and *nonverification* of any particular apprehension suffered in strand number 2. Both in private, intense interaction with the Zen Master (dokusan) and in exacting public participation in rigorous tests of authenticity (shosan), *all* apprehensions are struck against the community of those whose cognitive eyes are adequate to the transcendent, and such apprehensions are soundly nonverified if they do not match the facts of transcendence as disclosed by the community of like-spirited (and this includes past apprehensions once judged, by the standards of the times, to be true but now subrated or found to be partial by more sophisticated experience).[99]

It is with gnosis, then, verifiable gnosis, that our methodological repertoire is completed. And it is with gnosis that I end my informal sketch of a transpersonal sociology. For the final contribution that transpersonal psychology can make to sociology is, if you want to know about the actually transcendent realms themselves, then take up a contemplative-meditative practice (injunction) and find out for yourself (illumination), at which point the all-inclusive community of transcendence may disclose itself in your case and be tested in the fire of the like-spirited (confirmation). At that point, God ceases to be a mere symbol in your awareness but becomes the crowning level of your own compound individuality and structural adaptation, the integral of all possible societies, which you now recognize as your own true self. And when God is thus seen as the integral of all possible societies, the study of sociology takes on a new and unexpected meaning, and we all find ourselves immersed in a sociable God, formed and forming, liberated and liberating—a God that, as Other, demands participation, and that, as Self, demands identity.

References

The following is by no means a comprehensive or even representative bibliography. It is merely a list of those works directly mentioned or quoted in the text. I have included a short list of recommended reading in transpersonal psychology for those who might be unfamiliar with its basic tenets.

1. *A Course in miracles.* 3 vols. New York: Foundation for Inner Peace, 1977.
2. Anthony, D. "A phenomenological-structuralist approach to the scientific study of religion," chap. 8, *On religion and social science.* D. Anthony et al., eds., University of California, forthcoming.
3. Anthony, D., and Robbins, T. "From symbolic realism to structuralism." *Journ. Sc. Study Rel.,* vol. 14, no. 4, 1975.
4. Anthony, D., and Robbins, T. "A typology of nontraditional religions in modern America." Paper, A.A.A.S., 1977.
5. Arieti, S. *The intra-psychic self.* New York: Basic Books, 1967.
6. Assagioli, R. *Psychosynthesis.* New York: Viking, 1965.
7. Aurobindo. *The life divine, and the synthesis of yoga,* vols. 18–21. Pondicherry: Centenary Library, n.d.
8. Baldwin, J. *Thought and things.* New York: Arno, 1975.
9. Bateson, G. *Steps to an ecology of mind.* New York: Ballantine, 1972.
10. Becker, E. *The denial of death.* New York: Free Press, 1973.
11. ———. *Escape from evil.* New York: Free Press, 1975.
12. Bell, D. *The end of ideology.* Glencoe: Free Press, 1960.
13. Bellah, R. *Beyond belief.* New York: Harper, 1970.
14. ———. *The broken covenant.* New York: Seabury, 1975.
15. Berdyaev, N. *The destiny of man.* New York: Harper, 1960.
16. Berger, P., and Luckmann, T. *The social construction of reality.* New York: Doubleday, 1972.
17. Blanck, G., and Blanck, R. *Ego psychology: theory and practice.* New York: Columbia Univ. Press, 1974.

18. Broughton, J. "The development of natural epistemology in adolescence and early adulthood." Doctoral dissertation, Harvard, 1975.
19. Brown, N. *Life against death.* Middletown: Wesleyan, 1959.
20. Brown, D., "A model for the levels of concentrative meditation." *Int. J. Clin. Exp. Hypnosis,* vol. 25, 1977.
21. Brown, D., and Engler, J. "A Rorschach study of the stages of mindfulness meditation." *J. Transp. Psych.,* 1980.
22. Bubba (Da) Free John. *The paradox of instruction.* San Francisco: Dawn Horse, 1977.
23. Campbell, J. *The masks of God: primitive mythology.* New York: Viking, 1959.
24. Chomsky, N. *Problems of knowledge and freedom.* London: Barrie and Jenkins, 1972.
25. Clark, G., and Piggott, S. *Prehistoric societies.* New York: Knopf, 1965.
26. Deutsch, E. *Advaita Vedanta.* Honolulu: East-West Center Press, 1969.
27. Eliade, M. *Shamanism.* New York: Pantheon, 1964.
28. Fairbairn, W. *An object-relations theory of the personality.* New York: Basic Books, 1954.
29. Fenichel, O. *The psychoanalytic theory of neurosis.* New York: Norton, 1945.
30. Fenn, R. "Towards a new sociology of religion." *J. Sc. Study Rel.,* vol. 11, no. 1, 1972.
31. Freud, S. *The future of an illusion.* New York: Norton, 1971.
32. Gadamer, H. *Philosophical hermeneutics.* Berkeley: Univ. Cal. Press, 1976.
33. Garfinkel, H. *Studies in ethnomethodology.* Englewood Cliffs: Prentice-Hall, 1967.
34. Geertz, C. *The interpretation of cultures.* New York: Basic Books, 1973.
35. Goleman, D. *The varieties of the meditative experience.* New York: Dutton, 1977.
36. Greenson, R. *The technique and practice of psychoanalysis.* New York: Int. Univ. Press, 1976.
37. Guénon, R. *Man and his becoming according to the Vedanta.* London: Luzac, 1945.
38. Habermas, J. *Knowledge and human interests.* Boston: Beacon, 1971.
39. ———. *Legitimation crisis.* Boston: Beacon, 1975.
40. ———. *Theory and practice.* Boston: Beacon, 1973.
41. ———. *Communication and the evolution of society.* Boston: Beacon, 1976.
42. Hartmann, H. *Ego psychology and the problem of adaptation.* New York: Int. Univ. Press, 1958.
43. Hartshorne, C. *The logic of perfection.* La Salle: Open Court, 1973.
44. ———. *Whitehead's philosophy.* Lincoln: Univ. Nebr. Press, 1972.
45. Hegel, G. *The phenomenology of mind.* Baillie, J., trans. New York: Humanities Press, 1977.
46. ———. *Science of logic.* Johnston and Struthers, 2 vols., London: Allen & Unwin, 1951.

47. Horkheimer, M. *Critical theory.* New York: Seabury, 1972.
48. Hume, R., trans. *The thirteen principal Upanishads.* London: Oxford Univ. Press, 1974.
49. Ihde, D. *Hermeneutic phenomenology: The philosophy of Paul Ricoeur.* Evanston: Northwestern, 1971.
50. Jacobson, E. *The self and the object world.* New York: Int. Univ. Press, 1964.
51. James, W. *The varieties of religious experience.* New York: Collier, 1961.
52. Jonas, H. *The gnostic religion.* Boston: Beacon, 1963.
53. Jung, C. G. *The basic writings of C. G. Jung.* DeLaszlo (ed.). New York: Modern Library, 1959.
54. Kohlberg, L., and Gilligan, C. "The adolescent as philosopher." In Harrison, S., and McDermott, J. (eds.), *New directions in childhood psychopathology.* New York: Int. Univ. Press, 1980.
55. Kaplan, P. "An excursion into the 'undiscovered country.'" In Garfield, C. (ed.), *Rediscovery of the body.* New York: Dell, 1977.
56. Lasch, C. *The culture of narcissism.* New York: Norton, 1979.
57. Loevinger, J. *Ego development.* San Francisco: Jossey-Bass, 1976.
58. Maliszewski, M., *et al.* "A phenomenological typology of intensive meditation." *ReVision,* vol. 4, no. 2, 1981.
59. Marin, P. "The new narcissism." *Harpers,* Oct. 1975.
60. Marx, K. *Selected writings.* Bottomore, T. (ed.). London, 1956.
61. Maslow, A. *The farther reaches of human nature.* New York: Viking, 1971.
62. Merton, R. *Social theory and social structure.* Glencoe: Free Press, 1957.
63. Mishra, R. *Yoga sutras.* Garden City, N.Y.: Anchor, 1973.
64. Needham, J. *Science and civilization in China.* vol. 2, London: Cambridge, 1956.
65. Needleman, J. *Lost Christianity.* New York: Doubleday, 1980.
66. Neumann, E. *The origins and history of consciousness.* Princeton: Princeton Univ. Pres, 1973.
67. Ogilvy, J. *Many-dimensional man.* New York: Oxford Univ. Press, 1977.
68. Palmer, R. *Hermeneutics.* Evanston, 1969.
69. Parsons, T. *The social system.* Glencoe, 1951.
70. Piaget, J. *The essential Piaget.* Gruber, H., and Voneche, J. (eds.). New York: Basic Books, 1977.
71. Polanyi, M. *Personal knowledge.* Chicago: Univ. of Chic. Press, 1958.
72. Radin, P. *The world of primitive man.* New York: Grove, 1960.
73. Rank, O. *Psychology and the soul.* New York: Perpetua, 1961.
74. ———. *Beyond psychology.* New York: Dover, 1958.
75. Rapaport, D. *Organization and pathology of thought.* New York: Columbia, 1951.
76. Rapaport, D., and Gill, M. "The points of views and assumptions of metapsychology." *Int. J. Psychoanal.,* vol. 40, 1959.
77. Robbins, T., and Anthony, D. "New religious movements and the social system." *Ann. Rev. Soc. Sc. Rel.* 2, 1978.

78. ———. *In gods we trust*. San Francisco: Transaction Books, 1981.
79. Ricoeur, P. *Freud and philosophy*. New Haven: Yale, 1970.
80. Roheim, G. *Magic and schizophrenia*. New York, I.U.P. 1955.
81. Schuon, F. *Logic and transcendence*. New York: Harper, 1975.
82. Schutz, A. *The phenomenology of the social world*. Evanston: Northwestern, 1967.
83. Schutz, A., and Luckmann, T. *The structures of the life-world*. Evanston: Northwestern, 1973.
84. Selman, R. "The relation of role-taking to the development of moral judgement in children." *Child Development*, 42, 1971.
85. Singh, K. *Surat shabd yoga*. Berkeley: Images Press, 1975.
86. Smith, H. *Forgotten truth*. New York: Harper, 1976.
87. Sullivan, H. *The interpersonal theory of psychiatry*. New York: Norton, 1953.
88. Suzuki, D. T. *Studies in the Lankavatara Sutra*. London: Routledge and Kegan Paul, 1968.
89. Taimni, I. *The science of yoga*. Wheaton: Quest, 1975.
90. Takakusu, J. *The essentials of Buddhist philosophy*. Honolulu: Univ. of Hawaii, 1956.
91. Teilhard de Chardin, P. *The future of man*. New York: Harper, 1964.
92. Twemlow, S., et al. "The out-of-body experience." Submitted *Am. J. Psych.*
93. Washburn, M. "The bimodal and tri-phasic structures of human experience." *ReVision*, vol. 3, no. 2, 1980.
94. Watts, A. *Beyond theology*. Cleveland: Meridian, 1975.
95. Werner, H. *Comparative psychology of mental development*. New York: Int. Univ. Press, 1957.
96. ———. "The concept of development from a comparative and organismic point of view." In Harris (ed.), *The concept of development*. Minneapolis: Univ. of Minnesota, 1957.
97. Whitehead, A. *Process and reality*. New York: Free Press, 1969.
98. Whyte, L. L. *The next development in man*. New York: Mentor, 1950.
99. Wilber, K. "Eye to eye." *Revision*, vol. 2, no. 1, 1979.
100. ———. "Physics, mysticism, and the new holographic paradigm." *ReVision*, vol. 2, no. 2, 1979.
101. ———. *The Atman project*. Wheaton: Quest, 1980.
102. ———. "The pre/trans fallacy." *ReVision*, vol. 3, no. 2, 1980.
103. ———. "Ontogenetic development—two fundamental patterns." *Journal of Transpersonal Psychology*, vol. 13, no. 1, 1981.
104. ———. "Reflections on the new age paradigm." *ReVision*, vol. 4, no. 1, 1981.
105. ———. *Up from Eden*. New York: Anchor/Doubleday, 1981.
106. ———. "Legitimacy, authenticity, and authority in the new religions." Privately circulated ms.
107. Wilden, A. "Libido as language." *Psychology Today*. May 1972.
108. Zilboorg, G. "Fear of death." *Psychoanal. Quart.* vol. 12, 1943.

Recommended Reading: An Introduction to Transpersonal Psychology

109. Assagioli, R. *Psychosynthesis.* New York: Viking, 1965.
110. Benoit, H. *The supreme doctrine.* New York: Viking, 1959.
111. Campbell, J. *The masks of God.* 4 vols. New York: Viking, 1959–1968.
112. Fadiman, J., and Frager, R. *Personality and personal growth.* New York: Harper, 1976.
113. Goleman, D. *The varieties of the meditative experience.* New York: Dutton, 1977.
114. Govinda, L. *Foundations of Tibetan mysticism.* New York: Weiser, 1969.
115. Green, E., and Green, A. *Beyond biofeedback.* New York: Delacorte, 1977.
116. Grof, S. *Realms of the human unconscious.* New York: Viking, 1975.
117. Hixon, L. *Coming home.* New York: Anchor, 1978.
118. Huxley, A. *The perennial philosophy.* New York: Harper, 1944.
119. James, W. *The varieties of religious experience.* New York: Collier, 1961.
120. Jung, C. G. *Memories, dreams, reflections.* New York: Vintage, 1965.
121. Kornfield, J. *Living Buddhist masters.* Santa Cruz: Unity, 1977.
122. LeShan, L. *Alternate Realities.* New York: Ballantine, 1977.
123. Maslow, A. *The farther reaches of human nature.* New York: Viking, 1977.
124. Needleman, J. *Lost Christianity.* New York: Doubleday, 1980.
125. Neumann, E. *The origins and history of consciousness.* Princeton: Princeton Univ. Press, 1973.
126. Roberts, T. (ed.). *Four psychologies applied to education.* Cambridge: Schenkman, 1974.
127. Schumacher, E. *A guide for the perplexed.* New York: Harper, 1977.
128. Smith, H. *Forgotten truth.* New York: Harper, 1976.
129. Tart, C. *States of consciousness.* New York: Dutton, 1975.
130. Walsh, R., and Vaughan, F. *Beyond ego.* Los Angeles: Tarcher, 1980.
131. White, J. *The highest state of consciousness.* New York: Doubleday, 1973.
132. Wilber, K. *The Atman project.* Wheaton: Quest, 1980.
133. ———. *Up from Eden.* New York: Anchor/Doubleday, 1981.
134. Zaehner, R. C. *Mysticism Sacred and Profane.* Oxford: Oxford Univ. Press, 1961.

Index

Activity and passivity, 132
Adaptation, 105. *See also* Structural adaptation
Adolescent mood of active independence, 132
Adolescent separate-self sense, 134
Affects, 40
Agency, 38. *See also* Autonomy
Altered states, 5
Animals, 21–22
Annamayakosha, 52n12, 75
Anthony, Dick, 118–23, 127
    In Gods We Trust, 135–39
Anxiety, 94, 99
Apprehension, 156, 157
Achaic level, 70n
Arieti, Silvano, 71, 72
Atman Project, The (Wilber), x, 14, 15, 38, 75, 150
Aurobindo, 53n12, 74, 79, 100
Authentic religion, 1–2, 101–4, 115, 117, 120–22, 152
Authenticity. *See also* Deep structures; Legitimacy, vs. authenticity
    crisis in, 102, 124
    degree of, 102
    determination of. *See* Structural analysis
Autonomy, 7. *See also* Agency

Becker, Ernest, 93–95, 100
Belief, 105–6, 108

vs. direct experience, 5
Belief systems, 106–7, 148
Bellah, Robert, 27, 116–18, 121, 136, 137
Berdyaev, Nikolai, 74
Biofeedback, 131
Boomeritis (Wilber), 41
Borderline individuals, 149
Brahman-Atman, 75, 80, 90
Brainwashing, 136
Brief History of Everything, A (Wilber), 41
Brown, Norman O., 93
Buddhism. *See also* Zen Buddhism
    Mahayana, 104

Campbell, Joseph, 74, 95, 109
Cannibalism, 29–30
Caring, 7
Causal/ultimate level, 79–80
Chakras, 79
"Childhood Spirituality" (Wilber), 18–19
Chinese Maoism, 103
Chomsky, Noam, 91, 119
Christianity, 130, 131, 137
    Gnostic, 79
Civil religion, 103–4, 117, 124–25, 136, 137
Clan-cults, 133–34
Cognition, modes of, 141–42

Transpersonal psychology, viii–ix, 59, 138–39
Transpersonal sociology, 57–60
Transpersonal states. *See* Spiritual states
Transpersonal structuralization, 125
Transrational cognition, 75
Transrational vs. prerational engagements, 149
Transrationalism, xi, 36, 125
Tribal consciousness, 24, 25, 27
"True believers," 105–6, 108
Truths. *See also* Phase-specific validity universal, 38

Ultimate level. *See* Causal/ultimate level
Unconscious. *See* Consciousness, domains of
Union, 14, 24, 123. *See also* Oneness
Universal care. *See* Worldcentric care
Universal religiousness, 120
Universal truths, 38
Up from Eden (Wilber), x, 14, 21, 23, 25, 26, 28, 31, 33, 38–41, 95
Upper-Left quadrant (UL), 41–43
Upper-Right quadrant (UR), 41, 42

Vedanta Hinduism, 104
Vertical-emancipatory interest, 156. *See also* Emancipatory interest
Vertical growth. *See* Transformation(s)
Vijnanamayakosha, 52n12, 75
Violence, 29–30
Vision-logic, 77, 78

Warfare, 29–30
"We," 46
Werner, H., 114

Wholeness, original, 14
Whyte, L. L., 95
Wilber, Ken
    The Atman Project, x, 14, 15, 38, 75, 150
    Boomeritis, 41
    A Brief History of Everything, 41
    "Childhood Spirituality," 18–19
    criticisms of, 28
    Eye of Spirit, 23
    Eye to Eye, 16, 23
    Integral Psychology, 5, 18, 41, 42
    The Marriage of Sense and Soul, 41
    One Taste, 41
    "Pre/Trans Fallacy," 16
    Sex, Ecology, Spirituality (SES), 41, 55n17
    The Spectrum of Consciousness, ix–x, 37, 47
    A Theory of Everything, 41
    Up from Eden, x, 14, 21, 23, 25, 26, 28, 31, 33, 38–41, 95
"Wilber-5" model, 52n12
Wilber-Combs matrix, 18, 49n6
Women, psychology of, 7–8. *See also* Female values; Gilligan
Worldcentric care, 7–10, 12
Worldviews, 39
Wuthnow, Robert, 136–37

Yogic-saintly religions, 128, 131
Yogis, 78

Zaehner, R. C., 81
Zen Buddhism, 138
Zen Master, 157